Oklahoma Taxpayers' Guide: Taking a Stand Against the IRS

A STEP-BY-STEP PLAN FOR DEALING WITH TAX COLLECTORS AND UNFILED RETURNS WITHOUT GOING BROKE.

Marc Boulanger, CPA

Licensed to practice before the I.R.S.

1601 SW 89th Street, Suite D300 Oklahoma City, OK 73159
marc@summittaxrelief.com Phone 833-477-4911

Important Notice.

The two most important chapters in this book are chapter one on how dangerous it is to let the IRS get in your head, then chapter nineteen on life after tax problems.

Legal Disclaimers

This book is written to deliver accurate and authoritative information regarding the subject matter at hand. It should be understood that the author and publisher do not render legal, accounting, or tax services through this medium. The author and publisher shall not be liable for your misuse of this material. They shall have neither liability nor responsibility to anyone regarding any loss or damage caused or alleged to be caused, directly or indirectly, by the information in this book. The book is designed to inform you of the options available only. We highly recommend you seek professional advisors to assist you in determining which strategies will work in your unique and individual circumstances.

The stories of how taxpayers suffered, were about to give up, then found a solution, and now are living prosperous lives are all about real people. Some of these people are my clients; others are stories that tax resolution professionals around the country have shared with me.

The details, such as names and amounts, have been mixed up to protect the privacy of my clients.

Copyright © 2024 by Lonesome Cowboy Publishing In 7320 N. La Cholla Boulevard, Suite 154 #183, Tucson, AZ 85741. All rights reserved. No part of this publication may be reproduced, distributed, or transmitted in any form or by any means, including photocopying, recording, or other electronic or mechanical methods, without the prior written permission of the publisher, except brief quotations embodied in critical reviews and certain other noncommercial uses permitted by copyright law. ISBN 9798334125933

Table of Content

Chapter 1: What's The Worst That Can Happen? — 1

Chapter 2: Sometimes Bad Things Happen To Good People. — 10

Chapter 3: The Ten Best Strategies To Deal With The I.R.S. — 17

Chapter 4: What's The Inside Secret Of The IRS? — 22

Chapter 5: Can I Pay My Debt At 10 Cents On The Dollar? — 36

Chapter 6: What Are The Steps To Escape This Nightmare As Quickly As Possible? — 49

Chapter 7: What If I Did Not File My Returns Over The Past Few Years? — 57

Chapter 8: How Can I Find The Money To Pay The IRS? — 65

Chapter 9: What Is A Tax Lien, Levy And Garnishment? — 73

Chapter 10: What Are These Correction/Collection Letters I Get? — 78

Chapter 11: What Is The CNC (Currently Not Collectible)? — 83

Chapter 12: Is It Possible To Get My Penalties Abated? — 88

Chapter 13: What Is Innocent Spouse Relief? — 91

Chapter 14: Is There A Statute Of Limitations? — 100

Chapter 15: What Can Be Done With Installment Payments? — 103

Chapter 16: What About Filing For Bankruptcy? — 110

Chapter 17: Can I Change My Name Or Move To Brazil? Can I Challenge The Law? — 114

Chapter 18: Payroll Taxes — 119

Chapter 19: Will I Recover Financially And Get Back On Top? — 129

Forward

This book is for you if you are losing sleep because of unfiled tax returns or collection letters from Federal and State tax collectors.

You have rights. The government cannot run over you like it would 25 years ago. But you must have someone on your side that knows those rights and how to work with the tax collectors, so they have the least possible negative impact on your life.

Tax problems are not the end of the world. Millions of taxpayers have negotiated a settlement with the I.R.S. or State and got on with building their financial fortress.

When we get you out of this mess, your life will get better.

If you like, I will show you how to reduce your future tax liability by taking every deduction, tax credit and tax offset possible. That's how rich people get their net tax rate so low.

From now on, you'll become one of the best record-keepers in the country. It would not surprise me to see you at Costco running your office supplies and equipment on a separate credit card and separate receipt than your groceries. Co-mingling funds will become an error of the past.

From my experience, people who go through tax problems become aware that you must invest an hour or two in managing your finances and tax obligations every month. You will become that person.

Introduction

Bad things happen to good people. Dealing with the I.R.S. for past due taxes, unfilled returns, and unfair assessments is one of those bad things.

It's also scary; the I.R.S. publicizes harsh outcomes on purpose. They blast it all over the news when someone like Willie Nelson loses his Colorado vacation home, a local business is closed down, or Leslie Snipes goes to jail. They want you to be scared, so you'll be compliant.

Yet, most tax problems happen because you got hit with some unforeseen event that put you behind the eight ball. One small disaster leads to another, and pretty soon, you're getting letters threatening to clean out your bank accounts.

Today you have options; you can stand up to the I.R.S.

This book will explain how the government collectors work for income taxes and payroll trust fund deposits, with a step-by-step plan to fix those problems without losing everything you've worked for your entire life.

If you do not ignore the letters and phone calls, the outcome of a negotiated settlement is far less stressful than worrying about what might happen tomorrow. The truth is that the stack of collection letters you're hiding in the bottom drawer will not go away by themselves. Luckily, there are legal defenses and strategies to mitigate the impact of tax collectors.

If played well and you qualify, you may end up paying a fraction of what they are trying to get out of you. At the very least, we may obtain an extended payment period that does not put your daily life into hardship.

I know you don't want to lose your business and be unable to feed your family. I know you don't want to explain to your wife why the kids must live in a two-bedroom apartment because the IRS is seizing the house.

> **NOTE:** Worrying about what the IRS will do costs you more in health and income than the actual collection process. You'll see a common theme in this book, "Everything Is Going To Work Out."

Because of your tax-payer-rights, you can stand up to the IRS. Last year 2,000 families lost their homes to IRS foreclosure, and about 500 people went to jail. But those were the most notorious offenders. I've never had a client go to jail or lose their home.

You are not in that group. I know that because you're reading this book. The bad boys don't read IRS-certified letters; why would they read a book on getting past the collection process?

Get the problem behind you. Get professional help. The faster this problem is out of your head, the quicker you can return to building your family's financial fortress.

What we want to prevent is a long drug out financial collapse. It drains your energy at work and emotionally devastates you and your family. That's the kind of exhaustion that can lead to destroyed families. But it does not have to be that way.

Past-due taxes is a problem that requires experience. Getting help from someone licensed to practice before the I.R.S. who knows the law and how the collection process works is critical. You do not want to engage the collection agents on your own. It's far too easy to slip up and say something that can be held against you later or just to apply for programs or offer amounts that are not going to be accepted. It's common for the I.R.S. to ask for more information than needed, so they might find even more reasons to run over you.

Let your representative do the talking. The actor Wesly Snipes, who made an error in judgement in speaking to the judge right before tax evasion sentencing, bought himself three years in the slammer.

Hiring someone who can stand between you and the tax collector is far better than staying up nights worrying. That is why I wrote this book. To help you understand what you're up against and how to get past it all.

In the next one or two hours, you'll see how we can stop the collection letters, phone calls and asset forfeitures by facing the tax collector head-on. You have rights.

You'll read about the strategies and inside secrets others followed when they got hit with the same unfortunate events. You will learn how the I.R.S. looks at your entire financial situation before determining if you can make an offer-in-compromise and possibly settle your debt at 5 or 10 cents on the dollar.

Even more important, you're about to discover why the O.I.C. (offer in compromise) sounds pretty good when those slick salesmen call you on the phone and offer an easy way out. However, an O.I.C. can lead to unintended consequences that may haunt you for decades. DO NOT rush into a 'sounds too good to be true' phone pitch.

If the O.I.C. is inappropriate, we'll move to Plan B and get your debt classified as non-collectible or even work out a long-term payment plan that won't force you to live like a pauper in a Charles Dickens novel.

I've outlined the strategies and variables in this book that will determine the best way to get these tax problems behind you so you can get on with your life and maybe get a good night's sleep.

My office is local; we know many of the tax collectors that are making your life miserable. We have a pretty good idea of what they will accept and what fails to meet their guidelines.

Would you like to stop worrying about the tax man and finally get a good night's sleep? Invest one or two hours and read this book with the confidence that others have been exactly where you are, and they got through it. You'll read real-life examples of the legal and ethical ways to stop the I.R.S. from tearing your life apart.

If you have questions or would like to stop in the office for a chat, please feel free to give me a call.

Marc Boulanger, CPA, Phone 405-782-2300
Licensed to practice before the I.R.S.
1601 SW 89th Street, Suite D300 Oklahoma City, OK 73159
marc@summittaxrelief.com

At any time while you are reading this book, feel free to email me clarification questions.

Chapter 1:

What's The Worst That Can Happen?

Death and Taxes

The Piper Dakota airplane tilted to the north as the morning sun glinted off the windscreen. The pilot pushed the yoke forward, bringing the plane down to treetop level. The Pipers' airspeed was down to 60 knots, just a little over stall speed. The 53-year-old pilot knew it was unsafe to fly so low, but he had no intention of returning to the airport. As he skimmed over houses, parking lots and churches, he saw children waving from the school playground, but it didn't matter now.

Over the past three years, the I.R.S. had put Joe through the wringer. He lost his retirement savings; they drained his bank accounts, put liens on his home, and destroyed his financial future. Three years of constant anxiety had cost him his marriage and any chance of retirement or financial security. Joe could not see a way out; he was convinced the constant attacks would continue for the rest of his life.

Finally, Joe came to the end of his rope. He made the fateful decision to tell the world that he (and probably many other taxpayers) were treated unfairly. What Joe was about to do would be the ultimate tragedy, the worst possible outcome for anyone without hope. He decided to slam his plane into the second-story window of the I.R.S. office building just three minutes ahead and leave his wife and child behind. As the Austin, Texas, office building filled his windshield, he could not think of any other way.

That evening CNN and Fox News theorized that Joe might have been a terrorist, but I guess you have to sensationalize every tragedy if you want the ratings. In the end, Joe was just 'an average Joe' who got caught up in a web of complex rules and a relentless government agency that overwhelmed him.

I don't know why Joe found himself in the crosshairs of the tax collector. What I do know is that trying to deal with the most powerful government agency on the planet is enough to put the fear of God into anyone. Fear drives poor decisions. Joe needed someone to stand up for him, someone on his side who could show him that nothing is as bad as it seems.

After decades of going toe-to-toe with the I.R.S. on behalf of my clients, I can tell you one thing for sure: eventually, everything always works out unless you do something stupid.

It's been over ten years since Joe killed himself, and I still think about him when I meet clients trying to deal with the I.R.S. by themselves, or worse, those who ignore the collection agents until the problem explodes in their faces. The problem will not go away on its own; it just gets worse.

When Ernest Hemingway was asked how he went bankrupt, he replied 'well, it was slow at first, but pretty quick at the end." That's how the I.R.S. works, a letter now and then, maybe six months apart, but eventually, your name will boil up to the top of the list, and the hammer can come down hard and fast.

It's a terrible way to start a book

Reviewing a pointless suicide is a horrific way to start a book dealing with the I.R.S. No tax problem should ever get to the point of hopelessness. But it can seem like it when looking at tens of thousands of debt or maybe hundreds of thousands, with no idea how you will dig out from under it all. Or, as my doctor tells me, "A problem that can be solved with a checkbook is not a very big problem."

Money problems drive 40% of all divorces and 16% of all suicides. If that's not enough, the stress of tax debt can cause heart attacks and cancer. No research tells us how many of those health failure fatalities had tax problems as the underlying cause, but we can guess the number is probably over a quarter for people under 65. Owing the I.R.S. can flat-out drive your life into the ditch.

Letting tax debt fester drives us crazy with fear. Of course, they want you to be afraid. That's why you hear about all the sensationalized collection stories, especially around April 15th. Then, our media can be trusted to exaggerate the stories, so it sounds even more ominous.

People living in fear live terrible lives, have difficulty growing their businesses and have even more trouble at home.

But there is a light at the end of the tunnel. Most clients report they are back on their feet and doing well in a few short years after clearing up their tax problems.

I don't want you to suffer a total economic, family, or personal failure. It's far better to find someone who can step in front of the I.R.S. and prevent a complete collapse by intervening early and negotiating a reasonable outcome.

Will You Be Arrested?

Going to jail is very rare. In any given year, fewer than 500 people are sent to prison; that's only 0.0012% of all taxpayers. This figure is incredibly low when you consider the I.R.S. believes that 15.5% of us are not complying with the tax laws in some form.

People who do not file their tax returns or lie on their taxes may face jail time. You cannot, however, go to jail for failing to pay your taxes. Cheating on your taxes is a crime. Not paying your taxes IF YOU HAVE FILED A RETURN is not a crime. That is why filing is so important, even if you don't have the money to pay.

It may be possible to hide $500 here or there (DO NOT DO THIS!), but if the number you're hiding has a comma or even if it doesn't, you'll probably get caught. If the I.R.S. knows you are underreported, we can amend your returns and start working on a payout negotiation. Oh, and remember, they know more than you think.

NOTE: Going through the resolution process is far easier if you bundle up all the years you are behind and deal with it all at once. Let's get the mental anguish behind you so you can get back to building your life.

The I.R.S. Is Not As Harsh As It Used To Be But It Is Still A Best

About 25-30 years ago, the I.R.S. faced a string of legislation that flipped the collection process on its head. In the past, the I.R.S. could say you owed back taxes, and the burden of proof was on the taxpayer to show the assessment was wrong. You were guilty until you could prove yourself innocent.

The taxpayer rights legislation also cleared the way for tax resolution advocates (like me) that could take the taxpayers' side. Someone to act as a buffer between overzealous collection agents and average Americans tied up in a complicated system, often through little fault of their own.

The Tragedy That Tipped The Scale Against The I.R.S.

For the first 80 years of the I.R.S.'s existence, they grew powerful. As abuses in collections became common, Congressmen started hearing more and more horror stories from their constituents. Finally, the legislative branch realized they needed to reign in the I.R.S., or the system would collapse under public outcry.

The tipping point may well have been the suicide of Bruce Brannon, a 47-year-old attorney from Derry, New Hampshire.

(I hate to bring up another suicide, but when humans find their sense of hope ripped away, they don't think clearly.)

So the story begins when Mr. Brannon leaves his father's birthday party around 8 PM. on a warm summer evening with the explanation that he has to get back to the office to finish some work.

His New Hampshire home and Chatham, Massachusetts vacation home were under bank foreclosure because I.R.S. levies pulled all Brannons' cash out of the bank. He drove 100 miles to the vacation home, where he called his wife to tell her he would be working late. He then went into the garage, started the motor, and waited to go to sleep. Sleep for the last time.

The next morning, his mother discovered the body, clutching a handwritten note explaining that the I.R.S. just sat and did nothing while the local agent destroyed his career and life. He hoped his life insurance would cover his debts, but nothing else he tried seemed to work.

I don't have the complete details on what started the downward spiral. But it seems their accountant said it was OK to deduct the $80,000 they had recently lost in a recycling factory investment.

Six years later, the I.R.S. audits the Brannon tax returns and disallows the deduction. Then they asked for $225,000 with interest and penalties.

Writing off the $80,000 debt probably saved them $20,000 in 1986 taxes, but the I.R.S. wanted $225,000 for it six years later. I see this all the time; people have no idea how fast the I.R.S. piles on the little guy.

So in 1993, the I.R.S. wanted $225,000, but the economic downturn and losses in their real estate business had wiped out any reserves, and the Brannons could not pay the bill.

They made an Offer In Compromise in 1995, but it was rejected. Most of them are. The OIC is harder than your think.

What Mrs. Brannon discovered later as she sued the I.R.S. for excessive collection harassment made her cry. The I.R.S. internal notes said that if the Brannons had raised the offer by $2,620, it would have been accepted, but the agent kept it a secret.

> **HOLD IT RIGHT THERE:** If you are wondering what a certified tax resolution consultant does, I can see several things wrong with this story. First, why did the I.R.S. go back six years? They won't do that unless there is fraud or extenuating circumstances. Three years is the normal look back.
>
> If I was representing him, I would have raised issues about the agent going on some fishing expedition. I would have forced the I.R.S. to prove they had substantial reason to look back six years. Without that proof, the audit would have been limited. This entire scenario would have never happened. Mr. Brannon would be alive today.
>
> My guess (I do not know the situation; it is just my guess.) is that the Brannons started talking about the $80,000 deduction during the audit, which was enough for the revenue agent to start a fishing expedition because no one said STOP. The I.R.S. will act friendly, but they do that to trick you into saying too much.
>
> Then, why didn't the Brannons know about the $2,620 bump that would have pushed their O.I.C. through? They would have known when to keep pushing the negotiations. An experienced certified tax representation consultant never takes the first 'no' as the final result.

If you get audited, hire someone to do the interviews for you. If you try to settle your debt, find an experienced certified tax representation consultant that knows what the I.R.S. is probably willing to do to fix your case. I.R.S. will ask for more information than they need. You may well say something off the cuff that will get you in trouble.

Now remember that I'm telling you this story because it was one of the primary events that triggered the taxpayers' Bill-of-Rights legislation.

The collection efforts by the local office were so egregious that the agent involved left the agency. L.O.L., *yeah, I'll bet he didn't leave without a boot print on his bottom.*

Mr. Brannon was a lawyer in a small town; his reputation is all he has. But the agent went to all the local courthouses to find cases Brannon was working on. He then went to the opposing counsel and said, "If you settle this, I want the money. Don't send it to Brannon." The agent systematically destroyed his practice by destroying his reputation.

Then the agent started asset forfeiture actions without notifying the Brannons' so he could force them out of their home. His next step was to garnish Mrs. Brannons $500 a month part-time income working at the local library. They even took their teenage daughters' $300 savings account, money from babysitting, that she wanted to use to buy a car when she turned 16.

Dark times. Insomnia. Headaches. Tense stomach. Shirley Brannon became a skeleton from emotional stress. For their daughter, despite A's in Algebra I, Carrie Elizabeth failed Algebra II.

The final straw was the agent showing up when Mrs. Brannon was home alone and saying he wanted to do the appraisal on their home, poking into their bedroom and daughters' room. He even asked for six months of grocery receipts.

The pressure was too much for Brannon, and he finally took the final step, hoping it would bring the case to an end and spare his family. But it didn't. The I.R.S. even went after his life insurance money, expecting the widow Mrs. Brannon to live on $500 a month with her teenage daughter.

Luckily Mrs. Brannon sued the I.R.S. and went public with her story. It's rumored that Congressman Dan Rostenkowski even cringed when he reviewed the reports, which is funny because Rostenkowski was head of the Ways & Means committee for 13 years. It was on his watch that the I.R.S. became so harsh.

As Machevillie said in his Renaissance-era book "The Prince," no one gives up power unless it becomes too dangerous to continue being a tyrant. So today, we have a revenue service that will work with you if you get behind on your taxes.

In 1996 Congress passed a series of laws outlining taxpayers' rights and providing guidelines for agent behavior. Of course, it was too late for Mr. Brannon.

The conservative movement favored reform because they saw it as a way to curtail government overreach. The liberal movement voted for the measure because they knew that many more stories like the Brannons and America might rise up and demand the end of the I.R.S.

The I.R.S. settled the lawsuit without admitting guilt, made an undisclosed payment, and released all the liens, foreclosures and garnishments. But Mrs. Brannon and her daughter will carry the scars for life.

The taxpayer Bill-of-Rights put a lot of needed controls on the I.R.S. when collecting past due taxes, among other things. The law ensures due process when the I.R.S. collects tax debts. The agency must prove taxpayer liability.

Taxpayers can appeal I.R.S. attempts to lien or seize property to pay a tax debt. Before a decision, nothing can be done.

The taxpayer has 30 days to appeal the administrative decision to the U.S. Tax Court or U.S. District Court. Again, the I.R.S. cannot seize a taxpayer's property during court proceedings.

The I.R.S. must consider all payment options before seizing a taxpayer's home or business. The agency needs a court order to seize the primary residence.

If I.R.S. agents negligently violate tax code or collection regulations, taxpayers can sue. But without someone to stand up for your rights, you won't even know you can push back when the I.R.S. is out of line.

Summary:

If you find yourself in the I.R.S. crosshairs, my job is to be your advocate. To determine the best course of action among the many ways you can reach a negotiated settlement and to do as much as possible to reduce the impact on your family and finances.

With a certified tax representation consultant on your side, they will not leave you homeless and without a car. They will not sell your clothes or clean out your food storage. Your kids will not lose their PS5. But you will have a clean slate and a fresh start.

And please remember, in life, everything works out unless you do something stupid like taking your own life. Every one of my past clients got their life back together and surprisingly caught up financially after a few years.

Chapter 2:

Sometimes Bad Things Happen To Good People.

Most people who get behind on taxes did not mean to cheat the tax man. The most common way people get into trouble is when they get their return done, find they don't have enough cash to cover the tax bill, and then decide to put off filing.

It can take the revenue service several years before they ask for missing returns, unlike the bank when you miss a car payment, so we figure they forgot about us and just keep hoping no one notices.

Once you start down this path, it gets even easier to skip the next year's return and maybe the next year's as well. Catching up is a lot harder once you've delayed filing a return.

Everyone has bad luck from time to time, but the I.R.S. tax collectors don't care. If you depended on this year's cash flow to cover last year's tax bills, you are thrown between a rock and a hard place if something goes wrong. And believe me; things go wrong when we least expect it.

How do we get caught in the crosshairs of the I.R.S?

Tax problems rarely start with a taxpayer's intent to defraud the I.R.S. Most tax problem resolution cases begin with a serious life event that causes a tax issue. Tax issues can result from:

Divorce: Divorce tears apart dreams and families and can cause unpleasant tax surprises. In many divorces, the assets are liquidated to make cash disbursements. It's not uncommon for a spouse to be unaware that some property distribution payments are taxable. For example, selling your stocks to divide the cash may trigger capital gains or ordinary income tax liability. The family home sale will also create a liability, but a single person's first $250,000 is exempt. If a small business is involved, your cost basis (how much capital you put into the company at the beginning or borrowed over the years) is far smaller than the sale price.

A taxpayer may divorce near year-end and discover that taxes withheld from wages were based on filing a joint tax return with several exemptions. After filing as a single taxpayer, they find themselves grossly under-withheld and with a large, unexpected balance due. The taxpayer may be spending a lot to start over. Even amicable divorces can have these issues. When divorce turns hostile, other issues may make filing a tax return difficult. If enough animosity exists, one spouse may withhold tax documents needed to file a return or even destroy tax and business records.

Unemployment: During Covid, a young college girl that worked as a part-time waitress at my favorite restaurant got in big trouble. She worked two nights a week and made around $150 in total. When her restaurant was closed, she discovered she was eligible for over $800 a week between state and federal unemployment. It was a giant gift; she focused on her studies and living large on weekends. It was all fun and games.

Covid put a lot of people out of work, and the government was generous in unemployment compensation. However, they failed to tell anyone that the money was taxable. The government did not withhold taxes from Covid payments.

For those trying to get by on less income, taxes were the last thing on their mind. For people who saw their pay go up from the Covid checks, it all looked like free money and ignored the tax implications.

So taxpayers prepared their returns and found a tax balance due. So they mistakenly believed they should not file the return for fear of the I.R.S. coming down on them for the tax they cannot afford. That almost always leads to a three or four-year cycle of not filing. It ends when you start getting calls from the IRS.

The covid check is a tax resolution problem we're currently dealing with. It has been a few years, and the I.R.S. is catching up. They stopped most collection efforts between 2020 and 2023, but the gates are open again, and the letters and calls are coming with a vengeance.

Taking Money Out Of Your Retirement Plan: An old tax planning client of a business associate of mine was losing his business slowly due to tort lawyers suing him for broadcast fax advertising. It was sad because he was buying leads from another firm doing the faxing, but the lawyers did not care who was responsible; they wanted out-of-court insurance company settlements. So they sued everyone, guilty or not.

One day this client was so panicked that he did not have enough cash to make payroll over the next two months, and he felt sorry for his employees. So without talking to his CPA, he took the $100,000 he had in his 401k to make sure everyone would get paid.

Ultimately, all the employees lost their job anyway as the lawsuits kept coming and the business closed.

This client lost his pension. He then got the unexpected tax bill for $35,000, including penalties for early withdrawal on the 401k. And to top it all off, his laid-off employees let everyone in town know they hated their old boss for not paying them three months of severance pay after the company closed. They jointly signed a letter about it and got it into the local paper.

So it was one piece of bad luck after another, with a major personal sacrifice for his employees, and he was still hated by the very people he tried to help.

On top of that, this client still owed the taxes. The collection agent was aggressive and did not care that my client had collapsed his pension to put the money into the company so his employees would get paid. The good news was my business associate sent the collection agent all the financials, and since the total was under $50,000, they got him a five-year installment plan.

By the way, the client got back on his feet a year later and is now doing better than ever. However, I doubt if he will ever make another personal sacrifice for his employees.

Before making panicked decisions, ask your accountant for a second opinion. My advice would have been to close the company today because it will probably fail anyway and keep your pension intact.

Debt Forgiveness: Debt forgiveness causes tax issues too. After an economic downturn, taxpayers are often surprised to owe taxes. The I.R.S. taxes canceled or forgiven debt. Under the cancellation of debt rules, a problem that caused an asset to be abandoned, foreclosed, or repossessed can cost them taxes. Bankruptcy and insolvency are exceptions. Forgiveness related to a personal residence is an exception. But that rule changes, so check with your tax expert if your home mortgage is forgiven.

During the collapse of 2010, a client of another CPA I know with a $1,000,000 mortgage on his office building, which was in default. His tenants were going out of business left and right, and many had stopped paying rent. An investor offered to buy the building for $400,000 on a short sale. The bank approved the deal and forgave the loan balance, but on January 30th, he received a notice from the bank that the $600,000 of forgiven debt was income. That threw him into a tax resolution case he didn't see coming.

Business Reversal: Cash-strapped business owners may pay employees their net payroll without sending the I.R.S. the withholding tax. They view this as a temporary situation to preserve cash for suppliers and operating expenses. Using "I.R.S. cash" can quickly become uncontrollable. First, the I.R.S. delays detection, allowing the business owner to continue. Second, failing to remit funds to the I.R.S. incurs huge penalties, worsening the issue. The business may never recover after the I.R.S. begins enforced collection. The I.R.S. will pursue payroll trust fund delinquencies until hell freezes over or the ten years statute of limitations.

Health Issues: When you have a sick family member, taxes are not at the top of your list. Your family comes first. Yet, major health issues drain your resources, and you might be unable to cover your next tax bill. Cancer or mental health is one of those problems that no one caused, but you will suffer the consequences. Sadly the I.R.S. will not care.

After we get you through your current tax problems, I would like to meet with you for a follow-up tax planning meeting. During that time, we'll review setting up a tax-deductible HSA (health savings account.)

Even better, we might want to set up a MERP. A Medical Expense Reimbursement Plan allows employers to give their employees tax-free money that can be used only to pay medical expenses. It is an IRS-approved health plan or arrangement where an organization reimburses employees for out-of-pocket medical expenses incurred by employees or their dependents. All reimbursements are paid to the employee 100% tax-free if administered correctly.

Tax planning is beyond the scope of this book, but I would love to show you how to set up a corporation. You will then have access to a wide variety of tax savings strategies. We'll talk when your tax bills are finally handled.

Financial Misjudgment: Poor financial judgment may cause tax issues. In our business and personal lives, many things can go wrong, and you'll find yourself unable to pay your taxes. I cannot tell you how many times I've scrunched up my forehead and thought, "You did what?" while listening to a client talk about some business decision that will have a negative tax implication or put their wealth at risk. This one paragraph could be 3000 pages long. You did not set out to make a mistake; it's just that sometimes things go wrong.

Stock Options: Nonqualified stock options can create a mess. The worst cases were in the 2000 tech stock collapse (and again several times since). Let me tell you about how Karen in San Francisco got hurt. She exercised her options and made a healthy $130,000 gain. All on paper, she did not sell the stock; she simply exercised her option to buy the stock. However, in the 2000 collapse, many high-tech employees were surprised that exercising options that created an on-paper profit created a tax liability.

But then the market collapsed, and her stock went to 14% of what she paid for it in January of 2000. Carol was surprised to find out that she owed taxes on stock she had bought but had not sold. By March 2000, her total portfolio was only worth about $25,000 after the collapse.

Then she was told by her tax preparer that she owed taxes on the $130,000 gain at the time of exercising her options. The I.R.S. wanted her to pay taxes on the gain even though she did not sell. Worse, her total portfolio was worth less than her entire tax bill.

Generally, unsold stocks are not taxable until you sell; stock options issued by your employer are handled differently.

I know it is unfair that if your stock goes up, you owe taxes on the gain, but if it goes down and you sell, you can only deduct a small portion. You can carry the loss forward and take the max deduction again next year and indefinitely. For Karen, it would be 30+ years before she could use the entire loss. If she sold, her losses were tax deductible, but only at $3,000 per year – so she will carry that loss forward for a long time.

In the meantime, she was thrown into a tax default because her phantom gains triggered an unexpected liability.

As shown in the small samples above, most taxpayers with tax problems did not set out to beat the government.

Don't feel embarrassed.
Delinquent or unfair tax bills happen to everyone at one time or

another. You are not alone. National estimates range from 12 million to 24 million taxpayers are behind on their taxes at any given time. That's around one out of ten tax-paying households. (Remember that half the households in America pay zero income tax) Over our lifetime, half the U.S. population seems to have had an awful experience with the I.R.S. But it can be fixed.

You are not alone, and the agents at the I.R.S. don't care. You're just a case number to them, and they want to get it closed off the books as fast as possible.

The I.R.S. may be slow, but they never forget. If you miss car payments, 90 days later, you're taking the bus; if you miss your mortgage payment, you'll find your family sleeping at Motel 6 in about five months. But the I.R.S. will let you hang yourself for two, three, or even four years (while penalties and interest pile up) before they start hammering you for ALL the back taxes in full right now.

Summary:

Certified Tax Representation Consultants find that their clients are good people who unintentionally got in trouble with the I.R.S. Even those who have made mistakes but want to fix their tax issues deserve compassion and a second chance. An experienced practitioner can help troubled taxpayers navigate the I.R.S. maze with minimal conflict. This book will outline the details of what can be done.

Chapter 3:

The Ten Best Strategies To Deal With The I.R.S.

Our first and biggest goal is to keep any problems from getting to the point where the I.R.S. is filing liens, draining your bank accounts, or seizing your assets.

Now if I'm too late, let's move quickly to put the brakes on the collection efforts and try to devise a plan that keeps your life intact.

As you read this book, you'll find dozens of stories about people just like you with tax troubles. Every situation is different, and of course, the most popular idea is the offer in compromise, where you may get your total tax debt reduced by 90% or more.

Once the total picture is laid out, we can review these strategies and determine what works best for you. The important thing is not to delay because you want to maintain as much control over the outcome as possible.

> **NOTE:** You are NOT in control of the outcome if you do not open those letters and take the bull by the horns.

1. Replace substitute returns pushed on you by the I.R.S.

2. Pay the tax in full by selling property or borrowing.

3. Dispute tax on technical grounds

4. Get your debt listed as C.N.C. (currently non-collectible)

5. Installment agreements / the Fresh Start Program

6. The Officer in Compromise

7. Penalty abatements

8. Bankruptcy

9. Innocent spouse relief

10. Expiration of collection statute

Most tax resolution problems start with a failure to file, closely followed by an audit of past returns. We're going to cover an audit first.

In 2018 I had a client that swore the worse his audit could go was owing another $50,000. A year later, the number was $170,000 because the taxpayer was trying to resolve the matter on his own.

For no reason, he volunteered to take his family with him to a business conference in the Bahamas. He mentioned they rented their home out on Airbnb all the time, then he talked about a net loss carry forward from years ago and his accelerated depreciation.

I was not in the room during the audit; I wish I had been. I was brought in later to try to negotiate the $170,000 tax bill the client could not afford. Collection agents are trained to get you talking in hopes that you will give them clues on how to extract more money from you. I know the tricks and can play dumb if pushed into a corner.

Rule Number One: If you find yourself in an audit

Remember the number one rule at all times, **get professional assistance.** If possible, try to complete the audit without talking to an agent on the phone or in person. Here is another example.

Carol ran a small business out of her house as a broker for assisted living centers. She kept a list of all the openings and amenities around town for senior living homes. Concerned adult children would hire Carol to advise them on where to send Mom when she could no longer care for herself. Carol did OK and grossed around $220,000 a year with $125,000 net.

Her net was high because she ran the business out of her house, allowing her to be home with her children. She triggered an audit because her advertising budget was 35% of her gross. Healthcare brokers normally spend 35% of gross on advertising, but the I.R.S. red flag rules aren't always accurate or current. Red flags pop up whenever an expense is out of the normal range for a small business.

The audit started as a correspondence audit, simply looking for the receipts and proof of the 35% advertising cost, but the auditor decided to do a phone interview as well. So far, so good.

In one of the questions, the auditor said, "I used to run a business out of my home; I loved it because the kids could play in the corner of the room while I got my work done." She said it is such a friendly mom-to-mom voice that Carol replied, "Yes, I have a big window in my office with lots of light, and the kids often play board games or iPad in the corner."

The advertising deductions remained intact when the audit report came in from the I.R.S. a few months later. However, the $6,800 Carol had deducted for home office use was disallowed. The report stated that the office in the home was not used exclusively for the business. Carol accidentally told the auditor that her kids played in the room while she was working.

Just one sentence and Carol ended up owing around $3,000 in taxes, interest and penalties. **BE QUIET, if at all possible.**

This is just one of the reasons you should never handle an audit on your own. Carol would have paid her tax preparer about $1,000 to conduct the audit but ended up paying the I.R.S. $3,000.

Oh, and one more thing. Audit results are shared with the state. Since we have a state income tax in (Oklahoma), Carol got another notice about six months later asking for $300 more, including the penalties and interest.

When Carol called me about it, I advised her to pay the tax bill because going to war with the I.R.S. over a small amount is not worth the cost. When faced with a small tax bill, it is wise to seek qualified advice, someone who can give you a clear picture of the cost of battle and the chances of winning.

Why Is The Tax Code So Complicated?

In an era of tremendous partisan conflict on nearly every issue, there is one conviction that Democrats, Republicans, and independents all share: the American tax code is a complicated. But interestingly, it is our own fault.

Economists and tax professionals have long criticized the tax code's complexity as wasteful, inequitable, and ripe for evasion. According to Pew Research, 73 out of 100 taxpayers report that the complexity of the code is a problem for them. Policymakers from both parties have talked about replacing the current tax code with a simpler, easier-to-understand method for raising revenue.

Nonetheless, despite adjustments at the margins by the Biden, Trump and Obama administrations, this uniquely American tax system endures and isn't going away anytime soon. There are various causes for this, including political posturing, policy inertia, and lobbying influence over tax policy, to name a few. But arguably, the fundamental reason is that the public wants it that way, despite our protests about complexity and unfairness. We love our deductions.

The government wants you to own a home, save for retirement, invest in businesses, adopt needy children and even build apartments and office buildings. They encourage the desired behavior through the tax code to incentivize you to do what the government has decided would be best for America.

Comprehending the full meaning of that sentence is how anyone can use the tax code to minimize their tax obligations. After your past tax debts are cleared up, I'll show you how you can use the code to your advantage. The details are in the last chapter.

Providing incentives through the tax code to get the desired outcome is more popular than just writing checks to citizens. Politicians need to get re-elected, so they often take the easy way out.

Summary:

Clients who engage in tax planning at a higher level seldom run into problems requiring a tax resolution expert. The tax code is full of ways to reduce your obligations; we cover some of them in the last chapter of this book.

Chapter 4:

What's The Inside Secret Of The IRS?

If you understand how the I.R.S. works and what motivates the individual agents, finding an amicable solution to your tax problems is easier.

The common triggers that open a review of your taxes.

1. You failed to file your return
2. Your return is in error, and the I.R.S. wants it fixed
3. They believe you are underreporting your income.
4. You filed but did not include the payment

Now there is one more, and it's dangerous. If you are underreporting, you might get 'ratted out' by someone you know. It might even be one of those buddies down at the bar who heard you bragging about 'under the table' and were jealous of your success. We've also seen cases where a disgruntled employee, ex-wife, or business partner called in a tip to the I.R.S.

But most tax problems start when the I.R.S. computers believe something doesn't add up. Few come from phoned-in tips from people you know; I just wanted to warn you that it can happen.

When a new 'case' is assigned to the individual agents, they want to clear you from the books as soon as possible. In most situations, that means rushing the process to liens, levies, and garnishments as quickly as possible. They also want to ensure you pay as much money as they can get out of you.

Dealing with the I.R.S. can be perplexing and difficult. The I.R.S. wields considerable power, but you have rights if you ask for them. The most common types of audits are correspondence audits, the in-office audit, and the field examination.

The Taxpayer Compliance Measurement Program

However, before reviewing the three types of audits, I'll fill you in on the worst kind of audit you can face. It is called the TCMP audit or Taxpayer Compliance Measurement Program.

They use the TCMP audit or Taxpayer Compliance Measurement Program to determine the baseline for compliance and deductions.

To establish the averages for business expenses or charitable contributions and general compliance, the IRS initiates the TCMP audit. The I.R.S. is building a baseline on the average taxpayer's compliance and creating a database of average deductions to judge all returns. The results are top secret. It's strictly a random event if you get picked.

The audit is so cumbersome that legislation is being considered to compensate the 'victims' with a $3,000 tax credit.

DIF scores (discriminant function) are calculated by analyzing a large group (up to 50,000 randomly chosen returns) of intensive audits performed every few years. The primary goal of this sort of audit is to update the I.R.S.'s DIF scores. The I.R.S. will analyze every item on the tax return during a TCMP audit, and every component of the return must be substantiated by documentation. A TCMP audit takes a lot of time because a taxpayer must locate checks, invoices, contracts, bank statements, and other documents for the audit. Every line of the tax return is reviewed in a TCMP audit, so you must provide proof for all deductions, not just a few.

These audits are rare; I am telling you about them so you know how they can figure out if you are spending too much on advertising or entertainment. They also keep tabs on new ways to make hidden money. You may think you're clever by thinking of a way to avoid reporting income. You are not. Thousands of taxpayers have already tried what you may be considering doing, and the I.R.S. is already looking for you to try it too.

The IRP: They already know 95% of what you're doing

In my experience, the collection agent rarely asks a question they don't already know the answer to. That's because of the IRP. The IRP (information returns processing) system receives data submitted by employers, banks, 1099's and other third parties (payers like Visa and Venmo) reporting taxpayer income such as transfers, payments, wages, pensions, interest and dividends paid during the tax year.

The IRP process begins when the I.R.S. receives five billion monthly reports on money movement. These wage and non-wage information returns are then processed and prepared for computer matching with individual income tax returns.

From the time the I.R.S. begins to receive returns until the non-filler and under-reporter notices are sent to taxpayers, the entire process takes about 17 – 24 months. The match identifies cases in which taxpayers under-reported their income on tax returns or did not file returns at all.

95% of the economy is tracked electronically. When the auditor asks questions about assets at the beginning of your encounter, they know most of the answers. I guess they just want to discover upfront if you will try to hide assets or income.

I know your friends will tell you about under-the-table income and how they scammed the I.R.S., but you should know that most of that is barroom talk. The downside of I.R.S. problems is not worth the 25% in taxes you'll save on a few hundred here or there. Be honest and stay off the radar. There are plenty of ways to reduce your taxes that are IRS approved.

NOTE: Get someone like me to handle the agent interview for you.

Whatever audit you are faced with, it is always best to prepare and remain calm. Some simple audits can be over in a few weeks.

OK, now the three common types of audits.

The In-Office Audit.

That means you'll get a request to come to the local office and bring the documents and receipts the agent asks for in their letters to you. Don't go by yourself. My experience has been that many times, you can get these converted to correspondence audits if you ask. Not always, but often since Covid showed everyone that the in-person meeting is a relic from the past.

The Field Audit.

This is most common when your business is being audited. The I.R.S. will send a team to your location and ask for office space to conduct the review. That means your conference room might be tied up for a week or more. They will ask you to provide someone who can find documents, make copies, etc. The field audit is disruptive to your business operations. Plus, a room full of I.R.S. agents is scary to everyone in the company, and rumors will fly.

The Correspondence Audit

The correspondence auditing program is expanding. The letter most commonly associated with a correspondence audit is I.R.S. Letter 566 (C.G.). In these letters, the I.R.S. will ask questions about specific items on the tax return, such as income, expenses, and itemized deductions. The taxpayer should respond to the letter in a timely fashion. That means in the next two weeks.

Remember that if someone paid you money, you may not record that income, but the person who paid you did record the expense. So 95% of the time, there's a record of your income. That's a simplification but keep it in mind when you get the letters asking why your income was understated and you owe additional taxes.

Most of my clients who get these letters asking for less than $1,000 (and sometimes a little more) just go ahead and pay the money. I know it's unfair, but it will cost more to prove your point than the $1,000. I'm reminded of the opening monologue in the movie GoodFellas when Henry Hill says, 'Everyone takes a beating once in a while.'

Adoption tax credits caused a 100% audit rate.

A correspondence audit letter is usually a question about one certain item. For example, in 2011, almost 100% of everyone who adopted a child and took the legal adoption tax credit was audited.

I only had one client who took the credits. Their newborn son has been a blessing to that family, but in 2011 when the credit was new, the I.R.S. wanted to ensure it was not being abused.

In 2011 the law allowed for a $13,3600 credit. A credit differs from a deduction; credits allow a one-to-one direct tax bill reduction. My client was excited to hear about it; the private agency adoption ran over $50,000, so the credit was appreciated.

So the client got the one-item correspondence audit letter, and I talked to the agent for a few minutes on their behalf, rounded up copies of the $50,000 spent on the adoption and mailed them with the receipt requested/certified mail.

The entire audit was cleared up in a matter of days. I wish all of them were so easy.

The lesson here: If you take advantage of behavior modification tax credits like the adoption credit, or any of the 'green energy' home improvement credits, plan to be questioned. Save every receipt and make a lot of notes - you will probably need them in two or three years.

Remember what your mother told you, "Free money always comes with strings."

Some correspondence audits are big.

A few years ago, we had a CPA I know had a client whose corporation was domiciled in Wyoming (a good state for asset protection), but the owners lived 1,000 miles away. In 2014 they had a good year and reported a profit of 2.4 million, about 10x more than the average income for the past six years. That must have been enough to trigger an audit; the letter came in 2017. In the meantime, those 2014 profits were good enough to hit the clients 'enough-is-enough' number, and they started winding down the business and moved to Arizona to retire.

Normally, the audit might have been moved to the Arizona office, but I believe the auditor wanted the big case because it would look good on her annual review. Auditors don't get paid on commission, but they still need to look good for their bosses. This was larger than most, and I believe she wanted to look good.

So the auditor requested an 'in office' audit, meaning the client was being asked to travel back to Wyoming for an undetermined amount of time to go through the review process. The local C.P.A. that did their return was not interested in getting involved because he knew the taxpayer would eventually switch to an Arizona accountant. He felt it would be a thankless job for a retired client on the way out.

The CPA that was brought into the case by referral and immediately contacted the auditor to see if we could keep the client from traveling back to Wyoming.

They negotiated a deal where they would not protest the audit being done in Wyoming if they could move it to a correspondence audit so everything could be done by phone, fax, and mail. They also insisted that all communications were done through my office and that the taxpayers would only be brought in if it was absolutely necessary. They did not want to use the word subpoena because once the auditor starts filling out a subpoena, they may just keep adding pages and pages of information requests. It is important to keep the audit friendly.

Few people realize that you can negotiate with the I.R.S., especially if you understand the needs of the auditor or collection agent. By the end of the first call, the auditor got what she wanted, and the clients got out of spending thousands on airline tickets and hotels. They also got out of talking directly to the agent on the phone.

They were glad the auditor worked with the CPA directly because she did try to go on a fishing expedition by asking the company for the QuickBooks files for the past six years and a mountain of supporting documents.

One of the big advantages of a correspondence audit is that it's harder to say something stupid that will drag you further down the rabbit hole than you already are. With this family, they were able to take a list of what she wanted to see, argue against any overreach as they went along and then beg for 30 days before our next call when they delivered the requested information.

The client suspected they would end up paying additional taxes and wanted the audit to stretch out as they lined up access to credit.

I would love to tell you that the client left the audit without a scratch. However, it did not go perfectly, they got a haircut, but it could have been much worse.

Even though they controlled most of the audit process, the I.R.S. noticed that the client accelerated their depreciation without justification as they closed the business and paid some personal expenses with company money.

So, they ended up owing around $100,000. The client wanted to fight the amount, but the CPA reminded them they had also played with the inventory numbers and made a few other gray area business decisions that the auditor did not question. They told them, *"You got lucky they did not ask about inventory. My advice was to pay the $100,000 or risk the audit going deeper into your finances and possibly going back three* *or even six years to look for more."*

They were able to stretch out the audit and payment period to over one year. That gave the client time to set up a homeowner's line of credit and bring the audit to a close. They were lucky.

They needed the credit lined up before the I.R.S. filed any liens. Setting up a HELOC on a house with a tax lien is hard.

> **Tax problems do not count against your credit score,** but they do go on your public record. So, imagine you're a loan officer, and you see that public record. Your thinking, this guy doesn't pay the IRS, the most powerful government agency in the world and their employees have guns. If he won't pay them, he probably is not going to pay me. No loan.

Most correspondence audits are not that big. Most are simple questions about a line item on your return. They are fairly straightforward. Initially, the I.R.S. will send a letter to the taxpayer requesting information or explaining corrections and seeking the taxpayer's agreement to the adjustments.

Correspondence between the I.R.S. and the taxpayer is used to conduct the audit. The I.R.S. contacts the taxpayer to request proof for items listed on the tax return.

This happens a lot when your travel and entertainment expenses or your advertising cost are higher than other businesses like yours.

> **NOTE:** Save your documents. Today a scanner is so cheap, and online storage is almost free – it pays to just save everything. Now if you're wondering how long you should save documents, the new answer is until your dead or for at least five years. I heard one business owner that got nailed for over $200,000 in an audit because receipts and documentation from an NOL (net operating loss) from 18 years ago were long gone. Here is the kicker, the audit was on the final corporation return, two years after the owner died. The wife did not know where the 18-year-old records were, so the NOL was disallowed.

So if they ask why you spent so much money on marketing, you will need to send in copies of your contracts with the vendors and any supporting information you can find, such as a picture of an ad that ran or a copy of a sales flier.

If you are advertising online, simply print the reports from the Facebook ad manager. Then include a short letter explaining why it is customary for a business of your type to spend so much on getting new customers.

A no-change letter will be issued if the taxpayer's audit correspondence to the I.R.S. explains the proposed adjustment satisfactorily.

This is probably something you can handle yourself

If the taxpayer's information is not satisfactory to the I.R.S., a 30-day letter informing the taxpayer of the proposed tax changes and appeal rights will be issued. If the I.R.S. requires additional information, they will request it in writing from the taxpayer. If the second explanation does not resolve the issue, the return may be forwarded to a local office for further review.

My job is to get on the phone in a correspondence audit if it's going south and figure out how to keep it from being shifted to an in-office or in-the-field audit. Those are expensive for you.

Don't ignore those letters. If the I.R.S. does not receive an agreement or a response from the taxpayer within 30 days of the initial contact letter, they will issue another 30-day letter. If the taxpayer does not respond within 30 days again, a notice of deficiency will be issued, and the taxpayer will have 90 days to file suit in the United States Tax Court to contest the I.R.S.'s determination.

> **DO NOT IGNORE IRS LETTERS.** The quicker you respond the better the outcome will be for you.

What If They Find Prohibited Deductions?

The I.R.S. also has an Unallowable Items Program, which uses a computer to identify illegal items under the law. Some of these items are disability income exclusion; gambling winnings; foreign income earned; automobile expenses; medical expenses; federal taxes; utility taxes; automobile license, registration, tag fees or taxes; educational expenses other than taxpayer or spouse; charitable contributions as they relate to automobile expenses; business expenses as they pertain to automobile mileage rate; and casualty loss are the most common. There are more, but these are the most common.

Adjustments made under the unallowable Items Program are deemed to be the result of an examination, and the taxpayer is therefore entitled to a notice of deficiency and administrative appeal rights. When an unallowable item is discovered on a return, the taxpayer is contacted via correspondence from the I.R.S. Campus, and the necessary corrections are made. The letter sent to the taxpayer under this program requests that the taxpayer agree to the adjustments proposed by the I.R.S. and respond in writing with any disagreement.

If the taxpayer provides a satisfactory explanation, the case is closed. Otherwise, the I.R.S. retains the case for a correspondence examination. If an agreement cannot be reached, the I.R.S. will usually notify the taxpayer of his or her appeal rights. If no request for administrative appeal is received, a notice of deficiency will be issued, allowing the taxpayer to file a petition in the United States Tax Court.

What that meant was if you don't give them a reason why you don't owe the money in a timely and convincing manner, you will owe the additional tax.

One more story

Remember, you may ignore a money-in event, especially cash, but there is a good chance the transaction was recorded and tracked somewhere. Small transactions can slide under the radar but let me tell you about a client that did handyman work on the weekends.

Kyle worked hard every Saturday, fixing little things for people in his neighborhood. He always asked for cash. So far, so good, but then Kyle got greedy and deducted his business expenses against his main income. That triggered an audit. A few red flags popped up when Kyle tried to deduct business equipment and operating cost against a business showing zero revenue. The auditor had seen this trick before and made estimates on the income based on the expenses Kyle was deducting, and his day did not go well.

So here is an update. Kyle probably read somewhere that only 1% of the returns get audited, so he figured the odds were on his side. However, the 1% get picked by the computer because something smells like a dead rat. Kyle put himself in the 1% of returns that get audited by getting greedy.

I'm not telling you to cheat. But here is what Kyle could have done and probably gotten away with it for years.

Kyle should have absorbed his handyman expenses and forgotten about the tax deductions. Then when he collected that $300 or $400 every Saturday in cash, he could have used it to pay for entertainment, gasoline and groceries because his name is not on a receipt or contract. Even this stunt will become impossible in the future as facial recognition cameras will track you every time you go into a business.

That also means don't use a customer loyalty card and don't try to take a mileage deduction for your auto expense if you're paying for gas with untaxed cash.

> **NOTE:** A wise old grandfather once told me pigs get fat and hogs get slaughtered. Don't get greedy.

THE FINAL WORD - DO NOT CHEAT. Do not mix your personal expenses into your company account. Please do not buy a giant screen T.V. for the office and forget about it at home. The real problem with cheating is that it makes you think like a cheater, and it is hard to control dishonest behavior if we normalize it. Plus, who can sleep at night worrying about the I.R.S.?

If you have pushed the envelope in the past, keep your mouth shut. But let's walk the straight and narrow from now on, OK?

What happens if you do not file your return?

Because so much information about you is sent to the I.R.S. without your knowledge, it does not take them long to figure out if you failed to file. In non-filing cases, taxpayers are sent a series of notices requesting that they file their tax returns. Eventually, if you ignore the request to file, the I.R.S. will file for you. They will guess what you owe and start sending you collection notices. And guess what? The I.R.S. seems to be pretty good at rounding UP. You will not like the returns they file on your behalf.

Do you have to file missing returns

The answer is YES. When an audit starts, you'll get two questions in the first few minutes. A) Are all your past returns filed? B) What are your assets? Now they ask the second question to scare you because you start thinking about the family car, life insurance, pension funds and your home. All the things you've worked hard for over the years to provide for your family. You don't want to lose those hard-earned assets, so the questions play into keeping you cooperative.

But let's cover the missing returns. No audit or resolution of tax debt will get off the ground if the I.R.S. does not have all your tax returns in. If it is July and you file on the October 15th extension, they may let that one slide, but last year's returns must be completed now.

So my first steps will be to slow down the forced collection process and then get those past returns filed. Since we're doing them all at once, you'll get a discount, but they must be done; it's the law. Remember, it's not a crime if you don't pay your taxes; it is a crime if you don't file a return or lie.

Do you have to turn over your accounting software?

A favorite new trick is to ask for your QuickBooks backup files. You'll hear how this expedites the audit, and we can close your case quicker. Please don't believe it. You do not have to provide the raw data unless you are subpoenaed for your accounting software. Letting the I.R.S. dig around in your financial affairs for three years is a good way for them to find little things that can lead to bigger things. Simply say no or let us say no for you.

Send copies, not originals

Never, ever send the I.R.S. original documents. Always send copies and all correspondence via certified mail with a return receipt requested. The auditor will ask you to fax the documents but politely ask for an address you can mail them to. This gives you a receipt that your documents arrived, as the Department of the Treasury has previously lost documents and held the taxpayer responsible. I know it's unfair, but you must play the game by their rules.

Summary:

The I.R.S. knows 95% of what goes on in America because they get billions of reports about the movement of your money. That is why they know if you don't file a return or underreport your income.

When the computer system pops your return up, you start getting letters. Some can be solved in one phone call, while others drag on for a year or more, especially if you're in a complicated business situation.

When you're up next, the local agent has two main objectives.

    A) To get as much cash out of you as possible.

    B) To get your case closed quickly.

Our objective is to remove the emotional stress of dealing with the I.R.S. while doing everything possible to make sure tax problems do not disrupt your life.

Chapter 5:

Can I Pay My Debt At 10 Cents On The Dollar?

The Offer in Compromise (O.I.C.) is where we file all your back returns, add up all the taxes, penalties and interest and then make a discounted offer to the I.R.S. to get it cleared up and done with.

When you meet with a certified tax representation consultant, they will review your numbers to determine if your O.I.C. will likely get accepted. Sounds simple, but it is not.

Those crazy phone salesmen.

In 2015 at 10:45 PM, a client called me at home and said he had just gotten the strangest phone call; he wanted to know if it was a scam. It seems that a slick-talking salesman pulled him away from his family during dinner with news about a critical tax issue. The caller's I.D. showed a Miami phone number, and the salesman started talking about how he could get my clients' $150,000 tax liens paid off for ten cents on the dollar, and all it would cost was $4,995. The salesman then asked for my clients' credit card numbers.

Now two things came out of that surprise phone call.

A) My client did not even know about the $150,000 lien or what the caller was talking about. In my follow-up research, I found the lien was filed on an old abandoned "C" corp. that some other accountant had done the work for ten years ago. It had been years since the old company got mail, and the post office box was closed.

B) The second thing that surprised my client was that the salesman went right to an offer in compromise pitch and asked for $5,000. He would not take no for an answer.

Of course, my client hung up on the huckster but was so worried about the salesman telling him that if he did not do something today, the I.R.S. would take away the family home, capture his retirement accounts and garnish his wages. So he got me out of bed.

His first question was, "How did they know about a lien before I knew about it?" The answer is simple, once a lien is filed, it becomes a public record, and there are mailing list compilers who go through all the public records daily. As soon as your name pops up, it becomes a valuable commodity; the list compiler will sell it to a dozen 800-number salesmen in the next hour.

In turn, those salesmen start hammering the phone with scary predictions and high-pressure sales tactics within minutes. When they call you, they immediately start talking about the offer in compromise with the hopes that an easy way out will be enough to get $5,000 or more out of you in the next few minutes.

Well, some of these boys have a spotty reputation. We've had many clients contact us after paying the big dollars just to find out that one letter was sent to the I.R.S., and nothing else was done. It takes a year to get a ruling on an offer in compromise, and in many situations, those phone salesmen are long gone by then, regardless of the outcome.

So a year later, the I.R.S. is back after you but for an even bigger dollar number after more costs are added onto your bill.

Ten cents on the dollar sounds great, but as they used to say in the Ginsu knife commercials on late-night T.V., "Wait, there's more."

First of all, the O.I.C. is not always the right answer. For this client, I provided the agent with the last six tax returns and a list of assets. All of the values were zero. The corporation had been dormant for years. So, the clients' inactive "C" corporation was approved for C.N.C. status (Currently Not Collectable). I then told my client to let the ten-year statute of limitations run out.

The O.I.C. is the most common request I get from those who owe the I.R.S., so I'll give you a lot of insight into how it all works. Here is the good, the bad and the ugly of an offer in compromise. Then we'll go into the details of how to get approved.

The Good.

- An O.I.C. can provide you with a fresh start from your I.R.S. debt. It's especially effective if you owe more than $50,000.

- There will be no more worrying about the I.R.S. seizing your wages or bank accounts.

- Improved credit score - Following the completion of an offer in compromise, the I.R.S. will discharge all tax liens filed against you. Even better, we may be able to keep the O.I.C. off your public record entirely if we move fast.

- While the compromise is under consideration, I.R.S. collections are halted. After approval, you will be free of I.R.S. certified mail letters, I.R.S. Revenue Officer visits, and wondering what's next.

- Once the O.I.C. has been approved, and you are CONSISTENTLY making your payments. You can go back to making more money as the I.R.S. will not review the O.I.C. over the collection period. But if you fail to file one return or miss one tax payment, you are back to square one, and you won't like the outcome.

- You've put the I.R.S. behind you. Finally, you can sleep at night without worrying about what they might do to you next. It's over.

The Bad:

- You will still have to pay something based on your assets and income. The I.R.S. will determine if 'something' can be paid by you between five and twenty-four months. They decide but they do have specified rules that outline what an acceptable offer may be.

- Under penalty of perjury, you must tell the I.R.S. where you work, where you bank and what assets you have. They will know everything about your finances. That might include the diamond broach your grandmother left you 30 years ago.

- They are going to go over your financials with a fine-tooth comb. Remember, they already know 95% of what is going on in America (and most times offshore), so do not lie if asked a direct question. (It's better to let me do the talking.)

- The I.R.S. ten-year clock to collect from you stops running while an offer in compromise is being investigated. It might be wise to consider another route like the C.N.C. (currently non-collectible) so that you can let the clock run out.

- If they accept your offer, you must walk the line for the next five years. One missed tax payment or unfiled return, the O.I.C. gets canceled, and you are back to step one.

The Ugly:

- An O.I.C. is not a quick cure; it can take the I.R.S. at least 9-12 months to investigate, with another six months if an appeal is required; the I.R.S. then permits 5-24 months to pay the settlement.

- The I.R.S. has budgeting criteria that allow them to impose their will over yours.

- If you are untruthful about your income or assets during the application process, you are committing a felony.

- If the I.R.S. sees you have assets that could clear the debt, they may force you to sell them. This happens by rejecting your O.I.C. application and pushing for collection in full.

- The I.R.S. does not care about fairness; they want as much money as they can get out of you, and if they believe other collection processes will net them more cash, the O.I.C. will be rejected.

- Between 60% and 80% of all O.I.C. are rejected. That means they move back to garnishment, liens and sometimes foreclosure.

- Your chances of getting the O.I.C. approved are far better if an experienced tax resolution firm submits your application. The I.R.S. will automatically see that you have qualified help, making them feel better about your answers on the application.

Most taxpayers don't expect to get off scot-free; they want to catch up on the taxes, but the tax bill is so big that it has become impossible, even if you made $1,000 a week payment for the rest of your life.

Example of how the O.I.C. worked for one client.

Bob was a young building contractor who had not yet hit 30 years old. He had a wife and two children and was trying to grow his company a little too fast with the idea of building a future for his family.

He was borrowing on the last project to finance the next project and was way over-leveraged, mistake one. The good news is that his first two spec homes sold at top dollar, but he did not hold money back for the tax bill. Mistake two. He was so excited about the hundred thousand in profit rolling in that he started eight homes the following year, all on borrowed money.

Of course, you know how this is going to play out. Mistake three was the market turned, and his eight spec houses did not sell. The bank called his loans, and he lost everything, being forced into bankruptcy.

The family home went into foreclosure, and their little construction company failed. He filed Chapter 11 and was allowed to keep his F-350 (pretty old anyway) and some of his tools to get a job working for someone else.

They moved into an apartment on the wrong side of the tracks, and Bob started looking for a job.

Before the bankruptcy, a few of his vendors wrote off the balance due. He was surprised in February to start getting 1099s for the forgiven amount. Debt forgiveness, except on your primary residence, is considered income. Now debt forgiveness in bankruptcy does not create a 1099. Bob should have included the forgiven invoices in his Chapter 11 filing.

So now Bob has unrealized income, and the IRS wants him to pay taxes on it. Bob is in trouble because he is one of those rugged individualists who tries to figure out everything for himself to save money.

Bob operated as a sole proprietor because he did not want to pay an accountant to explain why he should incorporate his business dealings or advise him on his debt load and cash flow. The bank was happy that Bob was a sole proprietor; they wanted Bob on the hook if something went wrong.

In the meantime, Bob was so confused and heartbroken that he failed to file his taxes and that went on for a few years. When the I.R.S. caught up with him, he found out he was in debt to them to the tune of $175,000 because of the forgiven debt. They nailed him.

Now at this point, Bob has no assets beyond what he needed to make a living, and his income is just enough to pay for the apartment and groceries for the kids.

Bob is a prime example of when the offer in compromise is your best solution. Luckily Bob had learned his lesson about being a rugged individualist and doing everything himself, and he sought my help. When we finished filling out the financial position forms, it looked like the best Bob could do was $100 a week for two years. The good news is the I.R.S. accepted the offer, and Bob paid around $10,500 to wipe out $175,000 in taxes.

The I.R.S. did not want to take his old truck and tools because Bob needed them to make a living, and after all his family expenses, he had almost nothing left over for the I.R.S.

The even better news was that Bob finally had some financial advice and business coaching from my office, and he was able to start fresh.

Failure puts some people on a lifelong downward spiral. Bob took it as a lesson in how to become a real businessman, and as soon as he got the O.I.C. in place, he started working toward building his family wealth again. I am proud to tell you that he is back in business for himself, but this time he is not trying to get rich overnight. Now he is methodically building a solid foundation.

That is exactly what the I.R.S. wants. True, they want as much money as possible but don't want to destroy you. Bob will be a good taxpayer for the next 40 years because the O.I.C. let him get back on his feet.

The offer in compromise program allows the qualified taxpayer to clear up the past tax debt and start with a clean slate. The idea is to at least get some money out of you, bring you into compliance and teach you to be a good taxpayer from now on.

So don't screw up your second chance; you won't get a third.

Once we successfully get past tax debts erased at a discount, we sit down with our clients and explain how to keep better records, get their returns filed on time from now on, and budget the tax bills so this never happens again.

Our next meeting with Bob was to figure out how to plan his tax obligations year-round so he can use tax credits, qualified investments and better deductions to keep the tax bill as close to zero as possible.

How to qualify for the O.I.C.

You will not qualify for the O.I.C. if you have other means of paying your taxes or can qualify for an installment plan. However, it may become a legal option if you don't have the assets to pay the bill or if it would create severe financial hardship for your family.

The I.R.S. agent and your certified tax representation consultant will negotiate what severe hardship means. We'll try to get your payout as low as possible, but the I.R.S. has little tolerance for renting a cabin on the lake over the summer or a new F-350. So you may need to dial back your lifestyle for the next few years.

Just because you apply does not mean you'll get approved. Only 20% to 40% of the offers are accepted. Proposing an offer starts the I.R.S. on a process of verification and examination to fully understand the taxpayer's ability to pay and any specific circumstances that may further affect payment.

Finally, the O.I.C. seeks a solution that is in the best interests of the taxpayer and the I.R.S. Surprisingly, the I.R.S. would prefer to receive a portion of the outstanding amount rather than nothing.

THE ELIGIBILITY REQUIREMENTS FOR AN OFFER IN COMPROMISE

You must have filed all tax return paperwork to be eligible for an Offer in Compromise. That means back tax returns, any documentation about your current financial position the agent has asked for (they can ask for anything they want) and a check for 20% of what you're offering to pay. So if you offer $100,000, you will include a check for $20,000. That check will not be returned if your offer is declined. It will be applied to your tax-due account.

You must also be current on your tax deposits to be considered.

Offers are approved based on an examination of the applicant's particular set of facts and circumstances, which include

- the applicant's income
- your monthly expenses (some won't be approved)
- the applicant's asset equity. If you have $200,000 of equity in your home, they will want it.

These numbers determine how much you can raise by selling assets and how much you will probably earn in income over the next 5 to 24 months to pay your tax debt.

If you are involved in bankruptcy, your application will be disallowed. But Bobs' bankruptcy was over. You can learn more about bankruptcy in Chapter 16.

You should also make sure that any lingering innocent spouse claims or open tax audits are cleared up before entering into an Offer in Compromise. The I.R.S. has an O.I.C. pre-qualifier checklist that we'll be happy to provide you; just call our office at the number on the back of this book.

One last time, to make sure you understand, If you have assets, the I.R.S. will ask you to sell them. For example, if you own a $300,000 house with $200,000 of equity, they will figure you can get 80% of the value in a quick sale ($240,000), and after you clear the mortgage, you'll be able to send them $140,000. They will expect that money within five months of accepting your O.I.C. application.

Good news. Being forced out of your home seldom happens if you are in touch with the agent, answer their questions honestly and have a realistic plan to repay at least some of your debt. I will make sure you do all those things.

The R.C.P. or Reasonable Collection Potential

The I.R.S. expects me to submit a reasonable offer based on your real-life ability to pay them as much as possible. When they get an offer, they will run their own numbers, and if your offer is lower than what they think you can do, they will reject it.

Sometimes we can negotiate and offer a little more, but remember they only approve 20% to 40% of the O.I.C. offers. Our results for getting approved are much higher because we know what they will take and were experienced in presenting your case for review.

How do they come up with a dollar figure?

The I.R.S. determines the validity of your offer depending on your ability to pay. They start with your business and personal balance sheet and add up your equity in bank accounts, life insurance, real estate, automobiles, business equipment, jewelry, art and everything else that might be sold.

Then they consider your income. If you're making $100,000 a year, they will not consider an offer of $500 a month. Anyone who says you can't get blood from a turnip has never met an I.R.S. collection agent. They will squeeze you for every dime possible and a little more. I'll be at your side to protect you from any overreach.

The simple equation the IRS uses in your case.

Q.S.V. = Quick selling value, equal to 80% of the asset's fair market value. Since the market value is so volatile, I may have some back and forth with the agent.

MDI = Monthly disposable income, the money left over after paying for necessities. Keep in mind they will determine your necessities if we let them. They may decide that your kids don't need to go to private school at $20,000 a year; that money should go to taxes instead. Everything is a negotiation. However, they will not leave you destitute.

One-time payment offer. So the simple formula for a one-time payment (paid in five months or less) R.C.P. = Q.S.V. + (MDI multiplied by 12)

Now I'm sure you see the potential for failure here. They want you to pay your monthly installment based on 12 months of income, but you must write the check in 5 months. Keep that in mind when we negotiate your O.I.C.

So the total they will accept is the rapid sale value of your assets minus any mortgages or priority liens, plus your leftover income for the next year. Also, remember that in the lump sum offer, you must include a check for 20% of your offer; if you are rejected, they will keep your 20% and apply it to your tax debt.

Periodic Payment Offer Formula (payable over six to twenty-four months) R.C.P. = Q.S.V. + (MDI multiplied by 24)

This method necessitates multiplying the rapid sale value of your monthly disposable income plus your assets (jewelry, vehicles, property, etc.) by 24. If you go with the 24-month payout, you must immediately start making the monthly payments (no 20% down), even though they have not approved your request. If your offer is rejected, they keep your payments, of course.

A lump sum offer will be less than a two-year payout.

The periodic payment offer will give you more time to liquidate assets or borrow money against those assets or even make enough money from your business to cover the 24 monthly installments.

We'll do a spreadsheet on both options before making an offer so you can decide if it's worth the extra effort to keep that 57 Chevy you rebuilt or the lake house you're so proud of.

Either way, we will ask the I.R.S. to take a big haircut with the Offer In Compromise, and if we play it right and are honest with your ability to pay, you have a good chance of getting approved.

What if they reject my offer?

The easy answer is I will call them and find out why. Then if their request for additional information or a bigger payment number is reasonable, you and I will chat about the next step.

There are other alternatives to the O.I.C. You'll learn about them in subsequent chapters in this book.

What Are The Long-Term Consequences?

This question generally concerns getting back to your quest for building financial security. My experience has been that once the tax debt is off the table, you'll become a better steward of your money. Most of my clients recover in a few years and are back on track, but they are on solid ground this time.

That's because I will explain how to plan your taxes in the future. Smart people who spend an hour or two every month using the tax code to their advantage pay less in income taxes.

The second question is, 'What about my credit report?' I have no control over reporting your tax problems to the credit bureaus or how a bank or car dealer may look at your tax problems in the future. However, it is possible that if you move quickly and we get ahead of the collection agents, we might keep your tax problems and solutions off the public record. That will help you get back on your feet quicker.

Summary:

Offer In Compromise

An Offer In Compromise lets the taxpayer settle the entire debt by paying an amount that is less than what is owed. You must meet certain I.R.S. criteria to be considered; I'll figure that out for you. Once approved, you must file on time and make all your future tax payments. If you mess up over the next five years, the O.I.C. will be rescinded, and you will go back to square one.

The I.R.S. normally does not accept offers from applicants with the financial wherewithal to settle their tax burden in full through an installment agreement or by selling assets.

Advantages
- O.I.C. removes tax liens against the taxpayer in most cases
- As the debt goes away, you earn more money by not having to pay back taxes or think about the IRS collection agent.

- If you submit the O.I.C. before liens have been filed, keeping the entire plan off your public record may be possible.

Disadvantages
- You have to pay $186 as a filing fee to process the request
- A certain amount should be paid within 5 to 24 months to settle the debt.
- There is a possibility of the I.R.S. rejecting the request
- You must be perfectly tax compliant for five years.

The offer in compromise is a good plan to help you get a fresh start and become a lifelong compliant taxpayer. The reduced tax debt is especially helpful for those hit with massive tax debts because of unfortunate events.

Now I hate putting URLs in a book because they are hard to re-type accurately. But if you want to look at the assets and Q.S.V. rules, you can find them at

https://www.irs.gov/irm/part5/irm_05-008-005r

I'm sending you over there because I hope you call me once you see how complicated the I.R.S. rules are. We do O.I.C. applications every week, we have an excellent record of getting you approved, and it may be the right solution for your problem. Feel free to call me at the number on the back of this book if you have questions.

Chapter 6:

What Are The Steps To Escape This Nightmare As Quickly As Possible?

Randy received a collection letter from the IRS for $856 triggered by a disallowed deduction. He called his accountant and asked about the charge. His CPA explained that it would take three hours of work to pull up the return and review all the supporting documentation at $250 an hour and that, in the end, he would probably still have to pay the $856. The CPAs' good advice was, "Randy, just pay it and forget it."

Randy pitched a fit about unfair taxes and went yada- yada- yada for 10 minutes. Eventually, his CPA said, *"Consider your taxes a franchise fee for being able to do business under contract law. It's part and partial for the privilege of doing business in America. Just pay it, Randy."*

Randy got good advice from his accountant; even though he hated it, it was still good advice. I don't know, but my bet is Randy fired his CPA the following tax season because that $856 was eating him alive. That was foolish. The old adage is 'Don't sweat the small stuff, and it is ALL small stuff."

Remember the purpose of being in business. It's to do all you can to make it on Earth as it is in Heaven. That means being of service to others, starting with your family. Everyone gets hit with setbacks daily; if you let them eat you alive, you will never prosper.

When Should You Fix Those Small Tax Corrections?

So how do you decide when to handle the problem yourself, give the problem to your current tax preparer or get a tax resolution expert on board?

The answer is simple. In accounting, we use the term 'materiality.' Materiality means "Is the problem serious enough to make a difference?" For example, you won't have food on the family table or a place to live if the IRS gets everything they want; that's material. It does not mean you'll have to wait another month to afford the F-350 you've been looking at. If the problem is not material, pay the tax as soon as possible and move on.

Materiality Rule Of Thumb.

I tell most of my clients, "If your tax bill is under $5,000 and you have the money or credit card limits to handle it, just pay it." Be sure to tell your tax preparer next year about it, but for now, get the debt out of your life and out of your head so you can get back to work. Only you can set your levels of materiality.

What If You Don't Have The Money To Pay $5,000?

Call the phone number on your collection letter and ask to make payments of $100 a month. Ask if they will file a lien if you are making payments. They might ask for more but argue a little and try to keep it down. If you want to pay it off quickly, fine. But don't get into a bind a few months from now because the monthly payments are too high.

I recommend you have a list of your monthly expenses on an Excel spreadsheet before the call and offer to pay $100 a month. If the IRS wants to negotiate your offer and you are uncomfortable, give the job to your tax preparer. They may return with a bigger number and accept something in the middle.

Use Your Credit Cards If Needed To Pay Your Taxes.

If the person on the phone starts talking about lien, levy or garnishment, you want the $5,000 paid ASAP. Use a credit card to clear it off. You can search the Internet for "How to pay my taxes with a credit card" if you don't have cash. You will pay a 2% to 4% service charge. The IRS will not accept credit cards for payment, so it has to go through a 3rd party service.

For amounts owed under $10,000, you should work with your current tax preparer. Now if you owe $5,000 to $10,000 and are unsure why or even how you'd ever come up with that amount of money, then hire your tax preparer and follow their advice.

Most of the time, they will review the debt, probably agree with the findings of the IRS and then recommend an installment agreement as well, but they will have some advice on how to get the lowest payment possible. Getting approved for $100 to $500 monthly or even more is not a big enough problem to hire a tax resolution expert.

Bottom line: if you owe less than $10,000, all you need is someone to ask for approval of the Fresh Start program and negotiate monthly payments. Your CPA can handle that.

Does Your CPA Want To Handle A $10,000+ Resolution?

Unless they specialize in tax resolution, the answer is probably no. It may even be malpractice to take on a dangerous problem with a materiality level of impact on your life without specialized training.

You Have One Shot. Hire The Best Right Now.

It's like my family doctor; if he suspected I had heart trouble, he would immediately stop and get me into his buddy, that was a renowned cardiologist. Anything less is malpractice.

Resolution is a highly skilled specialty. Your tax preparer does hundreds of returns yearly. But she also does bookkeeping, payroll and helping clients run their business through advisory services. That's great, but it does not leave much room for learning the thousands and thousands of pages of instructions and case law concerning IRS debt.

If you find yourself in the crosshairs of the IRS for more than $10,000 or have not filed for two or three years, ask your CPA point blank. "Should I hire an expert?" Then call me.

What's The Step-By-Step Process I'll Use?

Step one: My first job will be to get a 'power of attorney' to engage the IRS on your behalf. I want to stop or at least slow down the garnishments, liens, levies, and property seizures the IRS has in store for you.

I'll contact the local office and explain that we're on the case and ready to clear the matter. The IRS loves the do-it-yourself taxpayer because you don't know your rights, and you don't know what they might agree to if you asked because you don't know.

The IRS will send you hundreds of pages of information on dealing with them in a tax collection or unfiled returns situation. But they will not advise you on the best alternative to get your bill dismissed, discounted, or delayed.

Remember, the collection agent has two objectives.

A) To get as much money out of you as possible.

B) To get the case closed as quickly.

It's in the collection agent's best interest if you don't know what you're doing.

However, when the IRS sees that you have hired someone licensed to practice before the IRS, they are even happier because we understand what the IRS needs from you. They now know your case will be handled professionally and will move to 'closed' status quickly. They know we'll advise on how to get the final negotiated settlement paid as soon as possible.

Step Two: We must find out the total amount you owe. If we miss a tax return or fail to report expenses or income, your settlement is invalid, and we have to start all over. It makes no sense to start working with the IRS, come up with a final number, and then find out additional taxes are sitting out there.

I'll request transcripts of your tax records. That means I will get copies of your old returns. I will also need to file any missing returns. The IRS will not settle your case if you have unfiled returns. But that might be a blessing.

Retroactively Electing To Become An S Corp. This One Strategy Saved Alan $25,000.

Alan came to me a few years ago and had not filed for four years. He ran his business thinking he had elected to be an S Corporation but had not done so in error, got behind on his quarterly deposits, and started ignoring the IRS. The first few deadlines are emotionally hard to ignore, but it seems to get easier as time passes, and no one calls you at home looking for your taxes. But we both know this will not continue forever, and it didn't work with Alan.

Alan ran a small construction business making around $100,000 a year.

The good news is that I could backdate an S Corp for Alan and file his business income returns through the entity as he had reasonable cause for the error. That means he saved $25,000 on payroll taxes over the four years. He should have been incorporated anyway, but it's a cute way to start from a lower taxes due number right out of the gate.

Now I am not recommending you don't file. Not paying your taxes is not a crime; failure to file a return or submitting false information on that return is a crime. Alan got lucky because I knew how to retroactively fix his business structure and code some of his income as dividends.

Step Three: The IRS will ask for supporting documentation, especially an audit. It's important to only give them enough to satisfy their questions. Many audits go south because the taxpayer sends in everything, including their QuickBooks files or the taxpayer talks too much. That is why you should not talk to the agent directly. I know I keep repeating myself on that one point.

When the IRS makes questionable determinations about the taxes owed, we may need to ask an administrative judge to overrule the local agent. I'll watch for this during any audits.

Step Four: Once we have the final numbers from the IRS, it's time to assess your financial situation. That will include assets, income, and your monthly expenses. That means all your cards FACE UP on the table in my office. Then we can create an offer and start the negotiations. I aim to get your tax liability dismissed, discounted, or delayed. I can keep the agency from driving you into poverty as long as they believe I'm being fair.

When I have all the details, you and I will decide on a strategy to get your tax debts behind you so you can start building your life again. These strategies will go from the offer in compromise to possibly getting your debt declared currently non-collectible.

Step Five: I will then present our plan to the collection agent. They want the case cleared off the books but also want to ensure you pay as much as possible. So, I have my work cut out for me. If appropriate, my position is that payment in full will create an undue hardship for your family. I'll lay out the case that what we are offering is as good as it gets.

I have a reputation for being a straight shooter with the collection agents I've worked with. That will help you.

Step Six: Once we have an agreement with the IRS, we'll get all the final paperwork completed and your first payments (if any) delivered to the IRS by certified mail. In some cases where your bills are considered currently non-collectible, I'll show you how to maintain that status until the statute of limitations expires.

Then we'll get the liens, levies, garnishments and seizures the IRS has in play closed out and removed.

Step Seven: In my experience, people who have gone through the tax resolution process prosper in their business going forward. With the pain and fear of the IRS gone, you can focus on what you do best and start rebuilding.

I'll advise you on rebuilding your wealth with tax-favored investments. If you want, we can start a tax planning process to reduce your taxes to as close to zero as possible. Plus, we'll review the requirements to ensure deductions are not disallowed, and you have the cash to make future tax deposits on time.

The most fun part of my job is laying out the playbook for your future wealth generated quickly.

Summary:

The real pain of dealing with the IRS is the fear of the unknown. They might swoop down and take everything you've worked on your whole life away from you. The outcome can be even worse if you accidentally committed a Federal crime.

The solutions are complicated on purpose; the IRS wants to collect every dime they can get their hands on. They have no mercy concerning your future beyond allowing you to live in a small, rented apartment and driving a ten-year-old car.

When I stand up to the IRS on your behalf, you have a fighting chance to survive and eventually prosper after the ordeal is concluded, and it will BE OVER sooner than you think, don't lose heart.

You've had setbacks all your life. Maybe you didn't get the first chair in the clarinet section; perhaps you failed to make 1st string quarterback. Maybe you did not get your dream job. In the long run, all those things were a blessing in disguise. So will getting through your tax problems. I'm here to help.

Chapter 7:

What If I Did Not File My Returns Over The Past Few Years?

Don't Panic; you are not alone. About 10+ Million people did not file their returns last year, about 5% of all taxpayers.

You'll remember from Chapter 2 that not filing is the most common reason people get into hot water with the IRS. For some reason, we get behind the 8-Ball, which is often beyond our control, and the burden of filing your taxes and paying out even more money is beyond our ability. So we just skip this year.

That turns out to be fairly painless; it takes them a minimum of a year to realize you're not going to file. So we often skip next year as well because we don't want anyone to notice last year's missing return. This becomes a cascading series of failures that eventually comes back to haunt you.

You will have to file eventually, or the IRS will file a return for you, and you will NOT like what they say you owe. But remember, everything always works out. The emotional pain of worrying about what the IRS will eventually do is greater than the pain of getting caught up.

FILE AND FIGHT WHEN YOU ARE DOWN ON YOUR LUCK

When I ask clients why they did not file for 3 or 4 years, they tell me about financial problems and being pretty close to broke. A common reply is, *"I was waiting until I got back on my feet so that I could clear it all up at once."*

STOP. If you want the best-negotiated deal from the IRS, you must look poor and you likely are at that moment in time. If you wait until you have $50,000 in the bank, they will go after it. If you have $500 in the bank, they will close your case under the OIC, CNC or low-dollar installments quickly, and the nightmare will be over.

> Getting back on your feet is much easier when your tax problems are in the rearview mirror. Don't wait.

Other reasons to get your returns filed ASAP.

YOU WILL LOSE YOUR REFUND AND TAX CREDITS. If you have a refund coming and fail to file, you will lose that refund after three years. You might also lose the earned income tax credit (or the other tax credits you may be eligible for) if you are four years late.

YOU CAN'T BORROW MONEY OR GET A MORTGAGE. If you don't have current tax returns, your opportunities for expanding your business or buying a home are greatly reduced because you won't qualify for credit.

YOUR NAME WILL SHOW UP ON THEIR COMPUTER SYSTEM SOONER OR LATER. Since the creation of Homeland Security after 9/11, the amount of tracking our government does of its citizens has gone through the roof. They already know 95% of what goes on in the economy, which means they know if you have a job, they know almost everything you bought and what you own.

You won't hear much about skipping a return for a while, but eventually, they figure it out. Somewhere between 12 and maybe even as long as 72 months, the IRS will start sending you letters. Please do not ignore them. It just makes everything worse.

THE BIG ONE. THE IRS WILL FILE FOR YOU.

If you did not file for the past one or more years, they figure you owe them money. But by law, they cannot initiate tax collection efforts without a dollar owed number. So they will file for you.

You are not going to like the return they file. They will estimate how much you make based on other sources like payroll reports, bank statements, the real property you own, eBay or Venmo numbers, and hundreds of other sources.

They will guess your income based on your home, car, bank balance and other assets and will even look at your social media to see if you have been bragging about all the places you have traveled to or the luxury car in your garage. When they file your return for you, they will round up.

They will give you your standard deductions but ignore everything else, like mortgage interest deductions. Your tax bill would scare the pants off a tailor by the time they are done.

IT CAN EVEN HAPPEN AT THE STATE LEVEL. This happened to a client of someone I know who owned a vacation house in California a while back. In 1999 he paid $4,000,000 for a house on the beach, and his family went there a few times a year. Except for a house sitter (to prevent squatters), the house was vacant the rest of the year. They did not put it on AirBnB because that did not exist in 2007 when our story took place.

The three weeks a year the family was in California, they did not earn an income; it was strictly a vacation home. Seven years after they bought the house, the state decided the client should pay California income tax because they owned real property in California.

The client refused to file; he told the collection agent from the state board of equalization, *"I do not have an income in California; I'm not a resident. You have no track record of a bank account or a paycheck for me in this state. All I have is a vacation house, and by the way, I already pay $40,000 a year in property taxes."*

The collection agent replied, *"Well, if you don't like our tax laws, maybe you shouldn't own property in California."* That escalated the conversation.

The tax collector was used to people cowering when he called, but he did not know this client. So at the end of the call, the collection agent was not very happy. This led him to file a $72,000 tax lien for 2007 income tax. Without notice, he just filed the lien. It was probably an illegal action because the state did not even send him a letter.

The client was not even aware of the lien; he found out by accident when he applied for a business loan and was denied because of the public record. So the CPA got the case and called the state of California.

The client hired them because he was so mad; he knew he'd lose his mind dealing with the state employees. When you are angry, you say things that do not help your case; that's another reason to use a tax resolution pro.

When they asked how they came up with the $72,000 number, they were told, *"In California, if you own a $4,000,000 home, you must make $750,000 - so the state tax on that amount is $72,000."* they were then told if they wanted the lien released, they had to file a state return. So they filled one with all zeros' and attached a letter asking about the legality of just filing a lien out of the clear blue sky.

Six months later, they got a release of the lien and two years later, the credit bureaus removed the public record. I'm glad the state of California did not audit the zero-dollar return, or that would have added a few thousand in cost to that client and another year of delay. I think the attached letter regarding the employees' behavior made the incident go away. You can stand up to tax collectors if you know the law.

By the way, that client never stepped foot in the state of California again. He sold the vacation home. Luckily, it sold fast because beachfront property is always in high demand. But to this day, if you use the word California around him, you will spend an hour listening to his opinion of California bureaucrats.

We can learn from all this: *"If the tax man wants to see a return, you better get it done, or they will make your life hell."* Even if you owe money, you don't have; it will be easier to work out the problem if you don't hold back on filing the returns.

SO YOU GOT A SUBSTITUTE RETURN, AND IT IS WRONG

You'll be notified that the IRS has filed missing returns on your behalf and that you have 30 days to file the correct ones based on your own numbers. If they don't hear from you, they will have another 60 days before they start collection efforts.

At this point, you really need to get into my office because we have to reconstruct your tax records by asking for the transcripts from the IRS (what they know) and then get the correct and probably much lower returns filed to replace the SFR (substitute filed returns).

Ignoring the IRS at this point is how people end up losing their homes, pensions, car and bank accounts.

GET EVERYTHING YOU MIGHT OWE ON A RETURN

When a friend of mine filed for business bankruptcy about five years ago, the lawyer gave him some solid advice. "I want you to throw everything on your list of debts and liabilities. If you borrowed $100 from your grandmother 35 years ago, put it on the list."

The idea was that once this event is over, we don't want someone coming back and making it hard for you again.

The same advice applies to your tax returns; at this point, the IRS is questioning everything you say. They flat don't trust you. From experience, they know that someone who does not file for a few years is the most likely to underreport income or exaggerate deductions. That's OK; we'll will do it right.

So if we end up going into an offer in compromise, we want to make sure we are compromising on the correct number the IRS can realistically ever come after you for.

WHAT IF I HAVEN'T FILED AND THE IRS DOESN'T KNOW IT?

Well, first off, they DO KNOW. They just haven't gotten around to you yet. Most people who come to me for past tax returns just found out they could not buy a home, get a security clearance, secure bonding on a big construction job or some other business opportunity because they don't have past returns.

If you need to provide copies of your past tax returns, know this one important point. You CAN NOT create returns and then give them to the bank without turning them into the IRS at the same time.

If the lending institution asks for copies of your past tax returns, they will verify them. That means they will ask the IRS for copies. Your loan will be disallowed if the returns are not on file at the IRS. Believe me; you're happy to get turned down in this situation. Plenty of folks are in prison for presenting fake tax returns to qualify for financing. That's felony fraud and messing with banks is a federal offense.

So here is the process. We will have to do some forensic research and paste together your income and tax-deductible expenses for the years you're missing. You may have the returns from your tax preparer and just didn't file them. That will save us a lot of work.

If we find out you owe taxes on the unfiled returns, you can include a check, or we can send them in without payment and start the process of negotiating a settlement with the IRS. That's a strategic decision to be made once all your cards are face up on the table in my office.

Our best option is to come to a repayment agreement between when the IRS gets your returns and when they file a lien or garnishment. With a plan on the table, they might not issue a lien on your assets. That is my goal.

KEEP YOUR PUBLIC RECORD CLEAN

We want to keep the IRS from filing a lien if possible. Even once it's been satisfied, it can stay on your credit report for up to 10 years. By law, satisfied tax liens cannot affect your credit score, but a lender can turn you down for any reason and seeing that public record might just be all they need.

EVERYTHING WORKS OUT

You've heard me say this over and over in this book. Almost every client I've ever gotten over the tax problem hurdle has come out better than ever after a few years. Even if you can't pay your taxes, you have not filed for years, and you have liens and on and on. Do not think your life is over.

Summary:

You will not go to jail because you can't pay your taxes. Failing to file or filing returns with false information gets people in legal trouble. The first choice of the IRS is to get the return, not ask for a prison sentence.

Catching up on unfiled returns will be uncomfortable, but it will be much less painful than waking up at 3 AM thinking about all the bad things that might happen to your family if the IRS brings down the hammer.

If we get ahead of the collection agents, we have a good chance of keeping your home, family, and business from disintegrating right before your eyes. That means getting into my office to start building a list of assets, income and liabilities. I can convince the IRS of a negotiated settlement on your behalf with truthful data.

Chapter 8:

How Can I Find The Money To Pay The IRS?

If you have no money and no assets and your job only makes enough for you to 'get by,' then we'll ask the IRS to forgive and forget. This is done with the offer in compromise or the 'currently non-collectible' petition.

You'll still have to turn in missing tax returns and go through a bunch of hoops, but the OIC will be the end of the pain.

I like the offer in compromise because it clears your mind and allows you to get back in the saddle working, but this time you'll do it by the book.

If you have more to lose than what you owe the IRS, we must find a way to pay them. Here are some ideas on how to raise the money based on what another small business owner was able to pull off.

Kirk was worried about his 2013 return because he crossed some gray lines when he fluffed up his overhead and depreciation numbers, then conveniently forgot some company assets he had sold. The CPA just pulled Kirk's numbers as is and did the return, which is what happens about 90% of the time. Tax preparers are compliance thinkers who use your numbers to give you an accurate return as they are permitted to use your numbers since they do not audit the information you provide them. If the numbers you give them are inaccurate, the tax preparer is not responsible for the outcome. That means you.

Anyway, let's get back to Kirk; He told his wife, "Well, we've gone 28 years without an audit, so the odds are in our favor. But, if we get hit on this one, it will hurt."

The 2009 recession had kicked Kirk and Sarah in the teeth, and they had not recovered. The tax tricks they pulled were justified in their mind because they simply did not have enough money to live on after four years of sucking down their savings. To them, the choices were to go into the gray area or learn to live without eating. So he signed the return, said a little prayer, and dropped it into the blue box outside the post office.

Three years later, the letter no one wants to get was lying on the kitchen counter. The IRS informed Kirk and his wife their return had been selected for audit. It did not even list why. It just said audit. When Sara asked, 'How bad could this audit go for us?' Kirk thought the worst-case scenario would be in the $65,000 range. They both looked out the window and sighed; where would they come up with that kind of money, they wondered?

I'll skip to the end of the story. The audit went worse than Kirk and Sarah anticipated, and they owed $160,000. It took 18 months for the audit to complete (because I stretched it out as long as possible), but they still owed 160k. It turned out that 2013 was not the only year Kirk had been depreciating construction equipment to zero as fast as he could and then selling the older tractors for cash out the back door without reporting the sale. So he got nailed.

At the end of an audit or resolution, you will have to come up with some money. You'll usually have 60 - 150 days to make the payment. We'll negotiate that for you because we understand what the IRS wants to see in your financial statements and what they are willing to accept. In the event of a successful offer in compromise, you may get two years to sell off your assets and clear the debt.

For Kirk and Sarah, our normal option of a monthly installment plan went out the window because the IRS will only do 'fresh start' workouts if you owe under $50,000. They are surprisingly easy to work with if that's your number.

We looked at the CNC (currently non-collectible). But Kirk was still making a little over $75,000 net, so a CNC ruling was also out. The CNC has to be applied for every year, and it will hang over your head for ten years until the statute of limitations runs out. I am hoping in 10 years, you're financially secure for life because of what you've learned about taxes and money during this ugly process.

Sarah wanted to do an OIC (offer in compromise) and offer 50 cents on the dollar, but I pointed out that you have 3 John Deere backhoes on the lot, you have over one hundred thousand in equity in your home, and you've got $56,000 in your retirement account. Your net worth is higher than your tax debt. The IRS will not accept your offer.

Sarah piped in, but we can't be in business without the backhoes; I don't want to lose my home, and that little pension is all we have in case we get old. I had to laugh under my breath on that one.

So Sarah and Kirk did not want to liquidate the few assets they had left after so many years of struggle.

Luckily, Sarahs' tax preparer had recommended she talk to me as soon as the audit letter arrived. He told her, *"Sarah, you need someone who has worked with the local IRS, who can strategically manage the audit for the lowest impact, and if you do get a big bill, he will be able to figure out some way for you to get out from under this."*

Kirk and Sarah needed time to line up credit or sell assets. It was a lucky break to get a client in the resolution process before the tax bill was assessed and liens started hitting their bank and the public records. They had a good credit rating, and we would need it.

We assess all the taxes due, income, and assets as part of the resolution process. So part of my service was to do an in-depth balance sheet of what they still owned after four years of just barely staying above water. For Kirk and Sarah, the positive side of the ledger, including equipment, real estate and pensions, came out to just a little over $225,000. So I turned to Sarah and said, "Plan for your tax audit to hit you for $225,000."

I thought I would get a black eye when she came out of the chair. So I quickly assured her, *"Sarah, I don't think you'll owe that much, but let's set that as our goal number for raising funds to get this behind us. If you don't need that much credit, no harm done."*

I will drag the audit out, so you have time to get ready. You'll have one year to line up the credit, maybe a little longer. Remember, it is far easier to borrow money now than after liens have been filed or your bank accounts have been seized.

We took the balance sheet and EVERYTHING that was an asset like equipment, accounts receivable, fixtures, the lease, life insurance policies, expected inheritance, the kids' college savings account, the antique pickup in the garage; I mean everything on the list.

We came up with two assets from the balance sheet that could work as collateral: their home and the equipment in the shop. The pension cannot be pledged against a loan by law. You can liquidate the pension, but you have to pay current income tax plus a penalty, and we want to avoid that at all costs. We'll just consider that a $56,000 insurance policy in case we fail at borrowing money.

We went over their credit report to make sure there were no surprises that might kill the plan halfway home. I updated their profit and loss statements and cleaned up the balance sheet. Once that was in place, I gave Sarah a list of places to start.

FIRST: Go to the two local equipment leasing companies in town and ask them to buy and lease all your equipment back to you. Please don't mention the tax problem; that won't be lying because until we get a final letter, you don't have a tax problem.

Your financials show a good business history, so this should work. Get bids from both, and we'll pick the best one. But there is one caveat. Tell them you're about to borrow money on your house and you don't want them to run a credit check, that you will be happy to sit down at their computer and run your own reports while they are sitting there. Running your credit reports does not count as a 'hard pull.' Too many hard pulls, and you look like you're getting ready to dash off to Brazil with other people's money. We need to keep that number to a minimum for now.

Sarah, you want a 100% valuation on the three tractors. Take auction listings of recent backhoe sales with you to demonstrate that you have $75,000+ sitting in the yard. You want $75,000 on a lease back for five years and a payout of $1.00 to get your equipment back.

You won't need the money for six months but want the deal done now so that you will be ready. This is because people in financial trouble never say, 'I don't want the money for six months.' That will make the local leasing companies feel comfortable.

If the leasing companies turn you down, we'll go to some local hard money lenders that love these deals, but their rates are high. (Raised $75,000)

SECOND: This one will embarrass you, Sarah, but you have to work every angle. Go to your landlord and ask them to defer one-half of your $2,000 rent for one year. Say to him, "We'll pay you the $12,000 you deferred over 48 months after we go back to $2,000." I would tell the landlord about the tax debt coming up and that you have to raise $225,000 in 12 months. Now your landlord will probably take this deal. Good tenants are hard to find; the half rent you're willing to pay him will cover his mortgage, and he will get paid in full overtime. However, don't agree to other liens because you've already guaranteed the lease personally.   Now take the $1,000 monthly in discounted rent and put it into a separate bank account.   (Raised $12,000)

THIRD: THIS IS THE BIGGEST ONE OF ALL: Go to a company called Fund and Grow in FL. They specialize in unsecured lines of credit for small companies by stacking credit cards. They charge around $4,000 to $5,000 to apply for 0% promotion credit card deals on your behalf. I've had clients get $75,000 on the husband's credit from 8 cards, then turn right around and get another $50,000 on the wife with six or seven cards. All at 0% promo rate for an average of one year.   But they will also negotiate with your bank for the HELOC. What you want is to be able to borrow the full equity out of your house. So they will ask for $100,000 on your behalf. They probably won't get everything you want, but they will get more than you can.   (Raised $200,000)

You should not do this one step at a time because your credit report will get hit with a lot of inquiries. You want that to happen on the same day, so it doesn't drag your credit rating down while you're securing money. Yes, this is legal. It's called credit card stacking, and several companies do it. I've just had a good experience with Fund and Grow.

As we already discussed, you can pay your tax debt with a credit card; you just have to pay a 2% to 4% service fee. Fund and Grow specialize in cards with a 0% introductory rate for six to twenty-four months.

In Kirk and Sarah's situation, they lined up $287,000 of credit and cash to cover the tax bill if the audit went bad. Luckily they did not need it all, but they were sure happy they had it lined up.

Every situation will be different, and your success will depend on how much time and initiative you have to prepare for the outcome. Remember everything on your balance sheet and all your personal assets can be used to secure financing if you're thoughtful about the process.

Sarah had one question "How will we pay back the loans?" Fair enough, so I pointed out that she would just have to increase her income after paying the tax bill. For the last few years, you've been stuck at $75,000 because you're under so much mental pressure about the 2009 recession and now this tax bill.

With both of these behind you, maybe you can finally start thinking straight again and pump up your income by $50,000 a year. That's only ten more jobs, so I know you can do it. If you dedicate the extra income over the next four years to debt reduction, you'll have all of this behind you.

Summary:

The purpose of this chapter is to review alternatives to tax resolution by finding a way to pay the tax debt in full by selling assets or borrowing money. The IRS will not accept a discount if you have income and assets, so in many cases, we just need to buy you enough time to raise the money.

Everything we talked about in this chapter is fluid. There is no way to tell what will happen, but if we plan for the worse, we can probably keep you afloat.

If raising money is not possible because you have no assets left, then we'll work on the CNC (currently not collectible) or an OIC (offer in compromise)

If you have liens and garnishments on your accounts, securing credit will be harder and more expensive, but it can be done by going too hard money lenders at higher interest rates.

The solution starts with knowing all the details, such as the total tax debt and what assets you have left. That requires some strategic planning. It's also a race against the clock; you must start planning for the final tax bill today. We've helped others find the money, so I'm confident we'll come up with answers for you as well.

Chapter 9:

What Is A Tax Lien, Levy And Garnishment?

During the tax resolution process, you'll hear some terms bantered about that you will need to understand. Liens, levies and garnishments are something we want to prevent. If you don't have to explain the IRS's actions on your public record, it's easier to get your life back on track after the tax problems are over.

If it's too late, that slows us down but does not keep you from getting the public record cleaned up as fast as possible. As soon as we come up with a payment plan, I will ask the IRS to release any holds they have on your assets.

Remember, you'll be a better money manager once you have this behind you. You'll recover your wealth pretty quickly.

In my negotiations, I'll make the case that your business will suffer, making it harder for you to pay the IRS back, so they need to remove the negative information. Sometimes it works.

If we put a payment plan in place and you default on those payments, the IRS will come back at you with the hammer of Thor, and I won't be able to get you clear of the liens again until the debt is paid off or the statute of limitations expires.

That's the biggest reason we go over how I plan to keep installment payments at a bare minimum by pleading future obligations and uncertainties. Of course, I never know in advance what reasoning I'll offer that comes from strategically reviewing your assets, liabilities and income in our first meeting. That means I might say, 'His car is old, and he'll need a new one in another year, you need to make sure he can make the payments. So don't ask for $1,000 a month, how about $300."

NOTE: Nothing you read here is going to happen without warning. You'll get letters and phone calls asking you to come in and negotiate a settlement long before the S*** hits the fan. Please don't go into that meeting by yourself, the IRS may sound helpful, but they are not your friend.

The three words are Lien, Levy and Garnishment.

Garnishment: If you've been in business very long, you've already dealt with a court order to withhold part of an employee's check and forward it to the governing authority. It's most common on child support but happens for unpaid tax bills as well.

The IRS will give you a warning that they are going to start garnishing your paycheck. Unlike most other creditors, the IRS does not have to get a judgment to pull money off your paycheck.

The maximum percentage the IRS can garnish your wages for is 25% of your disposable income. Disposable income is the amount of money you have left over after legally required deductions, such as federal, state and local taxes, Social Security, unemployment insurance and state employee retirement systems.

An example is If you earn $2,000 per week before taxes and other deductions are taken out, your disposable income would be $1,500 ($2,000 - $500 in payroll deductions). The maximum amount that could be garnished from your wages would be $375 or 25% of your take-home pay. For most Americans, that will make covering your mortgage or car payments impossible, so you DO NOT want a garnishment to go into effect.

When you get a notice of intent to garnish, get into my office so I can negotiate a more reasonable payment plan.

Lien: When you bought your house, the mortgage company filed a lien against it to put themselves first in line for repayment if the house is sold. The same thing happens on a car or equipment; it's pretty common.

From the IRS a Lien is not used to force the sale of property. It's simply an announcement to the financial world that the IRS has a position of interest in your asset, which must be cleared up upon a sale. But the bank that loaned you the money is first in line.

So if you sold your home for $500,000 with a $350,000 mortgage, the bank would take their $350,000 out of the proceeds. But if there is also a $200,000 tax lien on the property, the title company will forward anything left after the bank gets paid back to the IRS. You will get nothing out of the sale, and you will still owe the IRS. ($200,000 lien - $150,000 excess realized at sale = $50,000 still owed to the IRS.) The lien is released because you no longer own the house, but the remaining tax debt is still your responsibility. They will start looking for other ways to get the rest of their money.

Something Really Sick That Happened

The business owner (not my client) sold his shop building to help cover his taxes. He planned to sell the building and lease it back, a common way to raise cash. The building had increased in value over 20 years and would sell for a tidy profit.

However, when the building was sold, the bank and the IRS got paid (not in full), but the owner ended up with zero dollars. Then he found out that he would owe capital gains tax on the profit from the building sale, but he had no money left. This is a version of something called a *tax on unrealized gains*. It can keep the vicious tax collection cycle going to the point where it almost drives you crazy.

If it gets to the point where they are enforcing levies,' they might pull the money out of your IRA as well. Then guess who gets to pay the income tax and penalties for early withdrawals.

We can make strategic decisions on asset liquidations and loans that will keep you out of the traps. This is why having all the cards face up on the table is critical. In this sad story, I may have been able to negotiate with the IRS to leave enough cash in the deal to cover the capital gains or borrow the equity out instead of selling outright. My other option would be to recommend bankruptcy to deal with all the debts simultaneously.

Levies are different from liens. A levy is a legal seizure of your property to satisfy a tax debt. A lien is a legal claim against your property to secure payment of your tax debt. A levy is a legal tool to take your property to satisfy the tax debt.

If you do not pay your taxes (or make arrangements to settle your Debt), And The IRS Determines That A Levy Is The Next Appropriate action, the IRS may levy any property or right to property you own or have an interest in.

The most common example is a levy against your bank accounts. If your collections get to this point, you'll wake up some morning to the phone ringing. On the other line will be your foreman asking why his paycheck bounced and screaming at you about his own house payment will bounce now. What a nightmare phone call.

The IRS says they don't have eminent domain, but you could not tell from what I've seen them do. It is possible that special agents may show up at your door and take your wife's jewelry, or a tow truck shows up and pulls off your prized 1953 Chevy truck. By the way, special agents are the ones that have guns.

If you remember your first meeting or phone call with the collection agent, you went through a series of questions about your assets. Now you know why it was the first thing they wanted to talk about.

Don't lie. It is a crime to lie to a federal officer. They already know 95% of the answers before they ask the question, so it is risky to be less than truthful. They probably know if you have cash tucked away on a Caribbean Island. You will go to jail if you lie. But you don't have to answer either. You can get me on the phone, and I'll handle the inquiry.

Now the worst thing they can take is your means of making a living (your business or tools etc.) and your home. The good news is that they don't want either. Less than 2,000 homes are seized by the IRS each year in America. Considering the number of tax cases and the amount of worrying we all do about levy's' that's an amazingly small number.

I've never had a client lose their home involuntarily because I worked out a solution with the collection agent long before the problem went that far. Some clients did sell their homes to get out of the tax problem, but no one was foreclosed on by force.

Summary:

The wise thing to do is to get your cards face up on the table as quickly as possible with someone who is on your side. Come up with a plan to negotiate the amount or the payment schedule and then stick to the plan.

You'll get this horrible event behind you and enjoy a peace of mind that you probably have not felt for a long time.

Chapter 10:

What Are These Correction/ Collection Letters I Get?

The IRS increasingly uses computer-generated tax bills that are not really an audit. That means you can STILL get an audit after receiving an automatic correction/collection letter.

From 2020 to mid-2023, the IRS reduced the number of letters sent due to covid. The floodgate is open again, and you will probably be the victim of a correction/collection letter soon. We discussed this earlier in the book, but these are becoming so common that you must know how to manage them.

Now here is the kicker. The automated letter goes out if their computer system spots what it thinks is an error and recalculates your tax debt. Around 1 of 4 of these letters are wrong.

Why do they keep using the system with that kind of failure rate? Because it works. The average invoice is for under $600, and most people pay it. The truth is that is exactly what I recommend to my clients. If you pay me for two hours of work (I'll be on hold with the IRS phone system that long) to disprove the letter, my bill will be as much as the invoice. Let it go.

Now this is going to make you mad. It is estimated by Money magazine that the Internal Revenue collects over SEVEN BILLION in error because it costs more to argue than the bill cost. Sending out mistake letters and acting like it is God's word that you must pay is a money maker for them.

By the way, when an individual does the same thing and sends out erroneous invoices hoping your business pays it without thinking. That person will end up in Federal prison on mail fraud charges. Go figure.

The IRS is allowed to correct minor errors unilaterally by mail, but often they exceed the intent of Congress with some of their findings and calculations. The letter you might get falls into several categories.

Math Errors: The IRS claims your tax return contains math errors. For example, you listed four children for the refundable tax credit but did not put down their names. That is going to change your credit (refund.)

If their software misreads your number when it scans your return, you will probably get a tax-due notice, with your correction. They might also fix any other math mistakes they seem to find. But the truth is that the taxpayers make most of the math errors.

Penalty Notices: If you fail to file on time or make a payment by the deadline, the system will automatically calculate a penalty and ask you the amount due. They may abate the penalty if you have a reason you could not comply. You can write a letter back to the office that sent you the notice (attach a copy of the notice) and ask. Give them a good reason why the error happened.

You will probably get turned down if you have a history of non-compliance.

Interest Assessments: Late payments on any tax bill will generate automatic interest-due invoices. If you get the additional tax due set aside, you should also ask for the interest to be abated. They are normally pretty good at this; you should not have a problem.

Underreported Income: Now, this is the big one.

The IRS system looks for discrepancies between your reported income and income they learn of from 3rd party sources. The most common is a missed 1099. You probably reported the income on your return because you included any inbound checks or credit card payments in your sales numbers.

Remember, the IRS knows about 95% of what happens in the economy, and your debits and credits are someone else's credits and debits. That means when someone gave you money, they recorded it as an expense. It had better show up as income on your return.

The problem is that the numbers may not always match, or you recorded the income or expense in a different spot than the IRS expected. If they think something is wrong, they bill you for the additional tax and let you prove otherwise.

What To Do If You Get An Adjustment Letter.

First of all, my advice is to just pay the tax if the bill is under $1,000. It will cost more in aggravation and accounting fees than the taxes due. If the payment is impossible or the amount is larger than your pain threshold can tolerate, follow these steps.

Step One: Call the number on the notice and ask for an explanation. If you believe the IRS is wrong, ask for an abatement and offer to send written proof as a follow-up. Do that with copies of all documents, including the original IRS notice.

Step Two: Make your entire case again but in writing. Be kind, ask for help, explain why the IRS is wrong and ask for the adjustment to your taxes to be overturned. You have 60 days to get this done, do it ASAP because they don't open all their mail on the exact day it comes in.

Step Three: You can file to go to tax court. Now do not try to go on your own. The IRS will eat your lunch. They have 100 years of experience collecting taxes and have seen every trick in the book thousands of times. This will probably cost you $10,000, so don't go this far unless the number is big.

If you cannot pay the amount due, review the chapter on installment payments. The good news is that all this back-and-forth correspondence may buy you a few more months before you have to pay.

What If The IRS Does Not Respond

The people at the IRS love to keep reminding us how busy they are, how understaffed, and how sorry they are about not getting back to you. It can take them months to respond.

In the meantime, their computers will keep sending you the collection/correction letters repeatedly. Answer every one of the letters by sending them copies of your original request for abatement. Do not ignore letters from the IRS.

If you still have no answer after 90 days, call the taxpayer advocate at 800-829-4059. After you have explained that the IRS has not responded to your letters, they may be able to help you get the correction/collection effort cleared up quickly.

Summary:

In 2018 I was on vacation in Los Angeles and went to the Marina Del Rey to spend the day looking at boats I'll never be able to afford. I parked in a remote parking lot, paid my $50 bucks for the day and parked out at the far end of the parking lot. My mistake was that I backed into the parking spot to make it easier for my wife and kids to unload the truck with picnic supplies.

When we returned, a $200 ticket was on the window for backing into parking instead of pulling in. I looked around, and there was a sign in small letters at the entrance, along with two dozen other LA parking rules. The sign was 1,000 feet from where I parked, and I did not see it.

Well, I thought that was unfair, and I wrote to the city of Los Angeles asking for an abatement. They flat turned me down. I was a tourist spending a ton of money, and they did not care. I paid the fine and decided to just forget it. My favorite line from the movies is, "Everyone takes a beating once in a while."

Let the small problems slide if you can. Get your head back in the game of creating wealth for your family. It all works out in the end.

Chapter 11:

What Is The CNC (Currently Not Collectible)?

If you have very little income and almost no assets, I'll ask for your debt to be classified as CNC, which means currently not collectible. I'll give you two examples, the first is as big as a Lear Jet, the second the size of a Chevy Vega.

THE JET

In 2018 I walked into a business that needed an outsourced bookkeeper. When I arrived, I asked about the last bookkeeper and was told, 'Oh, she quit four years ago.'

They led me to the bookkeeping office and opened the door. The scene was right out of a something you would have seen on an old TV sitcom where someone yelled don't open that door." Too late, I found almost 100 banker boxes stacked to the ceiling; filled with invoices, receipts, and letters that never got opened. "How could you stay in business without paying attention to all this?"

Well, the owner explained. We started a new box on the 1st of every month, so all the boxes aren't full. But we just had an IRS auditor storm out last week when she saw this.

Yes, but how do you stay in business? The owner answered, "When people pay me, I just take the money to the bank, and I worry about paying my bills when the vendors call and threaten to cut us off. But I have not filed taxes since the bookkeeper left." So I think we're going to need to catch up. That's what the auditor told me when she left.

Well, the guy did not stay in business. His "C" corp. was in the trade of buying damaged private jets from insurance companies worldwide, repairing and reselling them. Most of his jobs were outside the USA, but he was a US corporation. It was the auditor that put him out of business, by the way.

She subpoenaed the bank records because the profit and loss statements were worthless and discovered they had sold several planes in South America. But the Columbian technicians only worked for cash paid in US Dollars and did not supply receipts, at least any the taxpayer could find.

So without proof of the expenses, the auditor declared the last two Jets sold at 100% profit. So gross sales became net profit - and the tax bill came in at two million.

So the business owner just quit doing business. He stopped buying used jets, and he stopped hiring contractors to work on those jets. He left $100 in the Wells Fargo company account. He filed zero zero zero tax returns.

He had no other assets besides a few desks and computers, which were probably worth less than $2,000 at liquidation.

He had already borrowed the maximum amount against his house and had no other savings, so he just returned the house to the bank. I mean, this guy was broke. That can't be a surprise; he had gone four years without doing any bookkeeping, he just kept running up credit cards and borrowing money to cover negative cash flow, and now it all caught up.

He didn't even file the four years of missing returns, letting the IRS file for him. He asked me what difference would it make if I owed two million or ten million. I can't pay either number, so I'm not going to pay you to reconstruct my records.

I did fill in the financial reports to show that the corporation could not pay anything, so he was classified as CNC Currently-Non-Collectable.

I liked this guy; he was fun to hang out with but not good at running a business. He explained that he operated as a "C" corporation because of the many tax-favored employee benefits available to him, but mostly because of liability. His corporation had no assets; it leased everything it used to run the business. If the company goes under, he just walks away. The audit put him under. He didn't even file bankruptcy for the corporation; he just let everyone have their judgments against an empty shell.

But Let's Go To The Chevy Vega Client.

About a decade ago, Manuel was a distributor for Kodak. His job was to fill the display racks at drug stores and tourist spots with camera film as well as secure new locations for the Kodak kiosk. He worked on commission as a W-2 employee for them.

Over time film sales dropped, and Manuels' income dropped as well. Kodak kept telling him that new tech was just around the corner and sales would be back up. *"Don't give up your route, or you'll miss the next big wave,"* they said. Well, the wave never came.

In the meantime, Manuel had collapsed his IRA and borrowed against his house to stay above water. When it all came crashing down, Manuel was left with a $70,000 tax bill, no equity left in his home, and no job.

He went to work selling landscaping for his cousin but only made about $35,000 a year. Yet the IRS wanted $70,000 right now from the IRA early distribution taxes and penalties.

With all the cards face up on the table, I could see that Manuel would not be able to pay. I went to the IRS and explained that he was currently filing his income tax returns because he was a W-2 employee and would stay current.

I also showed them his monthly budget, which left about zero dollars after feeding the kids and making payments on the house with all the equity borrowed. I explained that he had sold his truck and bought a Chevy Vega two years ago as his income went down and that he would have to buy another truck in the future or could not sell landscaping.

Currently Non-Collectable means you have no meaningful assets (they don't want your clothes or old car), and you only make enough to pay rent and buy groceries. They considered the grocery bill for five kids and the total house payments from both loans.

They awarded his case the CNC status. So he did not have to make payments on the $70,000. Manuel must ask for the status again each year as he files his return. He kept the CNC status for ten years, and then the statute of limitations ran out, and the $70,000 disappeared. The IRS released the liens on his house, and he was past the nightmare.

With the CNC status, Manuel quit worrying about the tax bill and focused on his cousin's landscape business. On a handshake deal, his cousin offered part ownership in the company (earned over several years) after Manuel could accept the asset without affecting his tax obligation. Under the law's strict intention, this was not legal, but it was all on a handshake between cousins, so no one ever thought to question it.

In the long run, the tax bill went away, Manuel ended up the half-owner of a great business, and his income was better than working for a big corporation. Everything always works out if you are not fogged over in fear about what the IRS will do to you.

Summary:

Only the IRS can allow the CNC designation. It only happens after your tax resolution advisor brings your assets and liabilities balance sheet and income statements to the IRS. If appropriate, I will make the case that paying anything would be an undue hardship to the family.

Negotiating your monthly payment to the IRS is NOT something you should do on your own. They will overcommit you, and you'll be right back in the hole in a few months.

Chapter 12:

Is It Possible To Get My Penalties Abated?

Last year a client came in a month late to do their tax return. I was pleased but reminded them that tax returns done in May would get hit with a late filing penalty.

"Yeah, I understand, but my dad died in March, and I was so busy with the details and trying to figure out where my mother would live that I just did not have time to get everything to you. I should have called and asked you to do an extension, but taxes were the last thing on my mind." He told me.

The next day, I completed the return and then reached into my bottom drawer and pulled out a penalty non-assertion request. By attaching the request for penalty abatement to the return, I prevented a string of letters and calls back and forth. The IRS accepted my request, and all was well.

Getting out of penalties is a lot easier if you've suffered a catastrophic failure like death in the family or your house burning down. Covid helped many people escape penalties, but that is over now.

You've heard of this on the news but probably never considered it. But from time to time, when there is a national disaster like the Hurricane Katrina floods in New Orleans. The IRS just gave everyone a penalty-free year based on their zip code.

The most frequently raised defenses against these penalties are death, serious illness, fire/casualty and natural disaster. Not working as well but seen in the past are erroneous advice, forgetfulness, and even ignorance of the law.

The erroneous advice is interesting because if you call the IRS and follow the directions they gave you over the phone, that advice happens to be wrong. You are liable for the penalties based on the erroneous advice the IRS gave you. Yeah, go figure.

Most penalties are based on failure to file and failure to pay.

If it is your first time, you will likely get a free 'get out of jail' card. It's a snap until you ask a second time. Then you'll have to ask your tax preparer to make some calls and write some pretty creative letters to get you off the hook.

So remember that you can get away without compliance the first time, but it will cost you after that.

SOMETHING CLEVER: I had a client that was notorious for not making quarterly deposits in his business. So he stopped taking a paycheck from his business until the last day of the year. In the meantime, he borrowed any money he needed from the business.

On December 31st, he wrote himself a $100,000 paycheck through the payroll service. Now if he had made 200k or 300k profit that year, he would have written a check to match the number. He wanted to get out of the quarterly deposit penalties.

It may be legal to pay yourself once a year. So on the payroll report, he entered gross pay of $100,000, employee advances to be repaid $75,000 and deducted the advances from the check. He then submitted the payroll. The $25,000 net paycheck was issued, but it all went to payroll taxes. He did not pay quarterly deposits but was clean in the eyes of the payroll company and the IRS.

If you pull off something like this, you better ensure you have the money in your bank on Dec 31st for those tax deposits. You need to talk this over with your tax preparer before you try this; it's the kind of thing that can trigger other problems down the road.

There are dozens of different penalties and just as many ways to combat the overreach of the collection agent. But there is little reason to learn about things that rarely happen. They did not file, and they did not pay penalties, make up about 99% of what I see.

If my request for penalty abatement is denied and the number is material, we'll ask for the case to be sent to an appeals officer. The IRS is still reeling from the Covid disaster and is so busy that we can often get a better ruling from appeals than I can from the collection agent.

Summary:

No one receives anything without asking. Penalties can be abated if we simply write a letter and ask.

Chapter 13:

What Is Innocent Spouse Relief?

Crying, she asked, *"How did they even know about the broach? It's been in my family for almost 100 years. My mother passed it on to me on her deathbed, just like her mother did. This is so unfair that I may have to give it to the IRS instead of my daughter. How did they even know it was in the safe?"*

June sat in my friends office in tears, trying to figure out how her husband got her into such a mess. The IRS agent had called and said, "You could sell that diamond brooch to clear up this tax bill."

Let's go back a few months and figure out why the IRS agent was on the phone in the first place. It turned out that Junes' husband had skimmed $48,000 from his business and failed to report it on their joint tax return. The IRS figured it out, and they wanted $17,000 in tax, penalty and interest. Since June signed the return, she was just as liable as her husband. The business wasn't doing well, and June did not work outside the home, so they did not have the money to pay the tax bill.

The wife was unaware that her husband had taken a 64 Impala SS Convertible in trade for a construction job and then sold the car a week later for $48,000 in cash to a local car dealer specializing in American heavy metal from the 50s and 60s.

Since it was cash, he figured he could pocket the money, catch up on a few bills, and buy a new compressor and welder for the family business.

Craig did not know that the transaction was recorded in detail on the books of the car dealer. The sales record included all of his personal information, including the social security number that the dealer required on the sales order.

Craig was shocked the following January 29th when he got a 1099-MISC from the dealer listing the cash payment. He called the dealer, but they brushed him off by saying, 'Too bad, buddy, it's the law.'

Craig did not want to put the 1099 on his return because he was hoping for a refund that year, not another $10,000 in taxes owed. Besides, he figured he had $48,000 in cost on that job, so the income was a wash, in his mind, so no harm done.

Well, the dealer reported the payment, but Craig did not report or attach the 1099-MISC. So the IRS did not see things the same way as Craig. They sent out a letter with an underpayment assessment that turned into a collection action when Craig hid the follow-up letters from his wife.

When the collection agent called June at home, the entire problem was a big shock. After a few days of disrupted domestic tranquility, she came to my office to see if anything could be done to save her jewelry.

My friend explained that if she was not involved in the bookkeeping for the construction business, and Craig did not tell her about the 64 Impala, there was a good chance they could ask for relief under the innocent spouse program. June did not want to lose that brooch as she was looking forward to giving it to her daughter when she grew up and had a family of her own.

As June got up to leave, she turned quickly and asked one more question "How did they even know it was in my safe?" Well, June, my friend said, I'll bet you have it listed as a line item on your homeowners' policy. These agents do a lot of digging before they call you.

The IRS has the legal authority and ability to find 95% of the income and assets in your life. They can subpoena anyone about anything at any time; when they ask you a question, they almost always know the answer before they ask. You are NOT notified if your bank or other business gets a subpoena with your name on it, so you never know until it is too late.

How The Story Ended

The IRS accepted June's request for relief, and we asked for an installment plan under the Fresh Start program. Craig was given five years to pay the $17,000 in monthly installments. Everyone was surprised he got 60 months, but they asked, and he got lucky. So as usual everything worked out anyway.

What Craig did was not out of malice; he was trying to clear up family bills and get equipment his construction company needed. The bottom line is he learned that the IRS is not a good bank to borrow from.

During the resolution process, my friend noticed that the record-keeping for the business was in shambles, so he was probably missing legal deductions and already paying more in taxes than he needed to. On top of that, his profit margins were below industry standards.

He and Craig started meeting once a month and worked on tax planning (which included getting him into an LLC instead of a sole proprietor status), how to bid on his jobs better, and controlling job costs.

Getting his business on track was much less work than getting June to understand how he almost lost her family heirloom, but I'm pretty sure they will be alright. It was a happy ending.

The Disappearing Wife, This One Was Off The Wall.

The next story is about how we lost an innocent spouse relief claim. But ended up negotiating a good deal with the local agent anyway.

Carl was going through the bookkeeper's desk and found a letter from the IRS claiming he had not made his payroll tax deposits for over a year, and the IRS wanted $165,000 in their office by Friday, or they would close his company and attach the assets.

How could this happen, he asked? First Sheila, and now this as he handed me a small, crumpled note

> *Carl*
>
> *The kids are at your mothers'. I am leaving you forever. You'll hear from my lawyer*
>
> *Sheila*

Whoa, this was going to be an awful experience for my new client.

I told Carl I would call the collection agent today and try to stop the business seizure. Then I will start digging around to determine what went wrong and see if we can save your business.

Well, the problem was bigger than Carl thought. The $50,000 quarterly income tax deposits had also not been made for the past three quarters.

It only took me one day to learn that Sheila (who is Carl's wife and full-time bookkeeper) had been scraping money out of the family business for a long time. I guess she planned to abandon her family and wanted her property settlement in advance.

It turned out that 14 months ago, she went into the bank and removed herself from the signature cards on the company checking account. No one noticed because all the bills were paid by online banking and credit card. Sheila had read somewhere that you can't be held liable for unpaid payroll taxes if you're not a signer on the account.

So every month, instead of making the deposit, she just used the online banking in QuickBooks to transfer the payroll tax to her private account in another city. She made adjusting entries in QuickBooks, so it looked like the taxes were paid, and since she got the mail and answered the phone, she intercepted any collection efforts by the IRS. Finally, when the IRS threatened to close the business, she slipped away. Sheila got out of her marriage and family obligations with $300,000 in cash that was supposed to go to taxes.

Carl never heard from Sheila again; he doesn't even know if she is alive or not. Of course, he filed for divorce, and the judge granted an expedited dissolution because of the unusual circumstances.

It could have been a lot worse, She did not drain the company savings account, and she didn't borrow any money using the company assets as collateral. The only other bad surprise was that she had used their family savings to pay the loan off on her car and took the remaining $30,000 in cash. Both were gone.

So Carl has two big problems. Well, he has more than two, but I only got involved in the tax bills. I went to the IRS and met with the collection agent using the innocent spouse's defense.

I laid out the entire problem, including a copy of the goodbye note.

We were able to show how we could make the payroll deposits going forward. That bought Carl a month before they closed the business. The collection agent could have been much less cooperative, but I think he felt sorry for Carl.

However, the agent wanted a plan on his desk in 30 days to repay the missing $165,000 in payroll tax if he was going to let Carl stay in business. He also told me to make sure Carl keeps current on all payroll deposits from today forward, or he will shutter the business without notice.

The IRS rejected the spousal relief request because Carl was in the office daily; he signed checks and was in the online banking occasionally. He was a successful businessman and should have seen what was going on. Remember, the agents are pretty skeptical about spousal relief.

The truth is, nothing about this case comes under the Innocent Spouse Relief, but I was able to reference the law's intention and catch a break from the agent.

To help Carl get things back on track quickly, I sent one of my employees, as a temp, to work at Carl's shop for three months as a bookkeeper. We did some forensic accounting and luckily found no additional theft.

Oh, by the way, I set Carl up on a payroll service, so the taxes were on direct deposit every month with the IRS. Not making your 941 payroll tax deposits on time is a dangerous game. This was critical to my 30-day plan to prove to the collection agent that Carl would not fall behind again.

Since Sheila was a 50% stockholder in the company, the police did not want to press charges saying this belonged in civil court. Even worse, the 50% ownership let the insurance company off the hook for embezzlement, and Carl was left holding the bag.

The family business was profitable, and I negotiated a payment plan of $10,000 a month to clear up the back payroll taxes. They abated the penalties but still charged Carl the interest. Overall I thought it was a good outcome. Pleading for innocent spouse relief worked because I went down to the IRS building and made the case for Carl in person. That's another advantage of hiring a local tax resolution expert. We have been to that office often.

We had the payroll tax problem under control, but that did not address the $150,000 in quarterly income tax deposits that were not made. On March 15th, Carl needed that money to cover his corporate tax return.

Embezzlement is a tax-deductible expense if you provide proof. But here was something tricky since the police would not file charges, and the insurance company said it was an inside job, I knew Carl would have a hard time proving the embezzlement if his returns were audited. Casualty losses are a big red flag for audits. I knew that dropping a $300,000 embezzlement on the tax return would have a high chance of triggering an audit.

I needed that casualty loss to get Carl's tax liability down so the police refusing to charge Sheila with a crime was putting us into a tough spot.

Carl was an emotional wreck during all of this. I tried to be helpful, but nothing would relieve the heartache and betrayal he and his two teenagers felt.

My best news was that he would save his business, and all the tax problems would be over in 18 months. I also predicted from my experience that this absolute disaster would be behind you in five years, and you would be a great father to those boys.

Summary:

This is a story of how the innocent spouse relief was not approved, but it may work for you anyway. Most people looking for innocent spouse relief are women who did not know the husband failed to pay income taxes and disappeared last year with his college-age secretary.

If the wife was not involved in the business or family finances, she has a good chance of being approved. Her chances are not good if she is driving a brand-new Lincoln Navigator paid for with misdirected tax money.

What is the innocent spouse relief provision

This strategy allows taxpayers to avoid paying additional tax, interest, and penalties if their spouse or ex-spouse failed to disclose income, reported income improperly, or claimed inaccurate deductions or credits on their joint tax return. If you filed a joint return with your spouse and your taxes were overstated owing to errors on your return, and you were unaware of the mistakes, you may request innocent spouse relief. Innocent spouse relief only applies to taxes owed on your spouse's earnings from employment or self-employment. You cannot seek relief for taxes owed on your own earnings.

Form 8857, Request for Innocent Spouse Relief, can be used to request innocent spouse relief. A request can also be submitted as part of a Taxpayer First Act petition to the United States Tax Court. If the request for innocent spouse relief is denied, the asking spouse may file an administrative appeal.

Pros:

- You may be able to avoid paying taxes on a joint tax return if your partner has made errors or committed fraud on the return.

- You may be able to avoid paying penalties and interest on taxes owed.

- You may be able to avoid having your wages garnished or your assets seized by the IRS for something you did not know or suspect your spouse did without your knowledge.

Cons:

- The rules are horrendous, and the IRS agent will start each case with a skeptical attitude regarding what the spouse knew or did not know.

- If you ask for spousal relief, it must be done within two years of being notified of the additional tax liability.

- If your spouse turned over ill-gotten gains to the family and you enjoyed the benefits of the profits, you will still have to pay the taxes, even if you did not know where the money came from.

Chapter 14:

Is There A Statute Of Limitations?

The IRS cannot collect on a tax debt forever. It will come to an end.

The IRS has ten years to collect tax debts from the assessment date when a tax return is filed, or an audit is completed. However, there are some situations where the statute might be extended. Here are some examples.

- The statute of limitations can be paused or extended by certain actions, such as filing bankruptcy, applying for an offer in compromise, requesting a collection due process hearing, or agreeing to extend the statute voluntarily.

- The statute of limitations does not apply to tax debts that are not assessed, such as unfiled or fraudulent returns. You are not on the ten-year clock if you have not filed.

- The statute of limitations does not prevent the IRS from taking other actions against you, such as filing a federal tax lien, issuing a levy, or garnishing your wages. These actions can affect your credit report, property, and income.

- You are pretty much stuck where you are if you're waiting out the statute of limitations. You can't show much income, you cannot borrow money from the bank, and you can't open an IRA and save money for retirement. They will grab any asset that shows up on the horizon.

- You might even have to delay taking your social security, or they may capture 25% of that.

It is far better to get a resolution to your tax problem than wait out the statute of limitations. There are occasions when it makes sense, especially if you have a "C" corporation without assets and no longer operating. We would have to review this because if the IRS determines you scraped off the corporation's assets to avoid paying the taxes, they will jump the corporate veil and go after you personally.

After ten years and under normal circumstances, the lien must now be removed if they have filed a lien against your property. However, it might stay on your public record, affecting your ability to borrow money for another seven years. You can ask for it to be removed from the public record after the statute of limitations has run out.

Sometimes that works because the IRS is so busy they may not reply to the request by the deadline. That does not automatically remove the public record; you must send a follow-up letter to the credit reporting agency asking for the removal. You have about a 25% chance of getting the lien off your public record in the year after your statute of limitations runs out.

Another Sad Story About Someone Who Did Not Seek Advice.

An old couple in Florida got in trouble when they sold some stock they had bought at $1.00 and ended up selling at a little under $850 per share eleven years later. They were so excited that they could pay for all 12 of their grandchildren to go to college that they sat down and wrote the checks to a dozen colleges the same day.

It never occurred to them they owed capital gains on the stock sale, and they did not even tell their H&R Block tax preparer about the windfall. As you might guess, about a year later, the IRS sends a letter asking for $200,000 in capital gains tax.

They did try to get the money back, but you know those Ivy League schools were not going to help. They were polite but stern, "Don't call us again."

The husband was so panicked that he insisted they sell their Florida home and pay the tax bill. The wife was mad; she insisted on hiring a tax resolution advisor, but the husband did not want to spend the money. She loved the house on the lake and did not want to leave. Did I mention she was mad?

About a year later, they were in one of those dinner seminars that estate tax planners hold, and the wife stood up and asked about the capital gains tax bill. She was still fuming over losing her house.

Without even thinking, the tax expert said, well, you could have ignored the tax; the only thing you own was the house, and the IRS would have put a lien on it, but in Florida, the IRS cannot force the sale of your home. The lien would have run out in ten years, and it would all be over. The tax bill goes away, and you own the house. Your only restriction is you could not sell the house for the ten years you had the lien on it.

The wife was so mad that at 71 years old, she filed for divorce the next day.

Summary:

There is a statute of limitations; it is a fail-safe, so you know the IRS will not keep looking under your skirt for the rest of your life. Sometimes we recommend using it, such as an installment payment plan that might only be $100 a month on a $100,000 tax bill. You pay on the bill for ten years, don't do anything to get the statute of limitations extended, and then at the end of ten years, it is over, and you end up paying $12,000 in total.

There are downsides; you may find yourself hamstrung for ten years from building your financial fortress because you must reapply yearly on those installment plans. When you start making money again, inherit a property, or build a business, they will come after you.

Chapter 15:

What Can Be Done With Installment Payments?

The IRS has something they market as the "FRESH START" program. It has a lot more to do with marketing than an actual program. It all boils down to the combination of everything we've discussed in this book. The Offer In Compromise, An installment agreement, Abatement of your penalties, and possibly the release of liens.

In some cases, we can get a lien released on your property before your tax debt is paid if I can show them that the lien is creating a hardship for you. So the bottom line is that "Fresh Start" is something to make you feel good about catching up on your taxes.

NOTE: If we can get to the IRS before they get a lien filed, we may be able to 'stop em at the pass,' as they used to say in the old westerns on TV. Your rebound to financial solvency will be easier if no one ever finds out you had a tax problem.

If calling it Fresh Start gets delinquent and probably scared taxpayers to get started, then the marketing terms worked. The Fresh Start is advertised to get non-compliant taxpayers to catch up on old returns, work out a payment plan, and keep current going forward. That is the ultimate goal of the collection agent.

The installment payment plan if you owe up to $10,000

It is probably best to go ahead and set up your own installment plan. The cost of bringing in a tax resolution service does not make sense for smaller amounts. Call the phone number on your collection notice and ask for the installment plan forms. They will ask that you include a list of your assets, expenses, liabilities, and income. Collection efforts stop during the negotiation process.

They will not let you go past ten years as that crosses the statutes of limitations, and the balance will not be collectible. The exception is the CNC notation that we covered in previous chapters.

If you miss a payment, the plan is canceled, and they will come back with liens, levies and garnishments, so stretch it out. Stay current on your tax returns and payments. Make your payments on time. And ask the collection agent not to file a lien on your public record.

Don't let the collection agent tell you what you can afford. They will not give you any wiggle room in the event of a future problem like a broken down car or rent going up.

Start low and argue every dollar they try to bump you. You need to set the monthly payment you can afford and do everything you can to keep them from bumping you up to a number you may not be able to cover in six months for some unknown reason.

If you owe $10,000 to $50,000 to the IRS,

Suppose your tax bill is over $10,000; hire a tax resolution expert. The IRS will push you into payments that are too high and, in most cases, be less than truthful about what they will accept.

My job as your representative is to look at your entire financial situation including potential future obligations and unanticipated calamities. Then I will negotiate the best deal for you. The danger is getting into an agreement, finding the amount too high, and defaulting. If you default on an installment, all bets are off, and they will not be nice.

The IRS will charge a small fee to set you up on all installment programs, somewhere between $31 and $225. If you are below the poverty line for your family income, you can ask to have the setup fee waived.

They will push you to pay the total tax bill within the ten-year time limit. However, if you cannot do that and they have no other reasonable course of action, we may end up paying $200 a month on a $50,000 tax bill. That means that you ended up paying $24,000 plus interest over ten years. The debt is forgiven at the end of ten years, and any liens are removed from your property.

Remember, they will tell you the installment plan must be paid in full in ten years. But if $200 a month is all they can get, then that is all there is. They will negotiate, and if you understand what they will actually accept, you'll come out better than on your own.

The Release Of Liens

At the end of your agreement, the release of liens (if we could not stop them at the pass or get them removed) is supposed to be automatic. Still, as you might guess, the government is not worried about your individual money problems, so I might have to remind them to forgive and forget.

In an installment plan, interest and penalties will continue to accrue.

Once your installment plan is in place, there is no need to let them have more money than we need to. They will likely keep any tax refunds you have coming during the installment period. Nothing I can do about that, so make sure your withholding and deposits are right on your best estimate of how much you will owe in taxes.

Congress designs that money to help lower-income people buy groceries and pay rent. We may be able to petition them to release your low-income and child tax care credits. If you qualify for that extra refund, I will have to force the issue each year to get the check issued.

It is possible that the IRS may review your installment plan from time to time, and if they feel you are capable of making bigger payments, reassess your obligations. We will argue against it if the amount is significant enough to justify the cost.

My objective when deciding between the Offer in Compromise and the installment plan (or the other options) is to keep your important assets out of the hands of the collection agent. I don't want them to get your home, pension, or ability to make a living. You'll need those assets after we get you through this mess, so you can rapidly start rebuilding your financial fortress.

Installment Plans if you owe over $50,000

In 2019 I talked to a potential client who did not hire me. He felt he could negotiate with the IRS directly. He owed $300,000 after an audit that went back six years. He was pretty distraught as he was in the middle of applying for a $300,000 home improvement loan. The family wanted a barn and swimming pool, and Dad was excited to make it happen.

When he asked about the installment plan, he was told it was for people who owe less than $50,000. Well, yes, that's true, but the collection agent did not mention that installments are available for higher amounts as well, just under a different name. The omission of information is exactly why you should never go up against the most powerful government agency in the world by yourself.

The client ended up paying the tax bill in full using credit cards. He took on the debt because he did not want a lien on his public record and did not want to lose his home. Now the potential problem with using credit cards (you'll remember we talked about credit card stacking, is that if you don't have the $300,000 in cash when those 0% promo rates expire in a year or two, you are going to end up paying 15% to 21% interest on the cards. The interest alone will exceed the installment payments if you had chosen to pay the IRS directly. But it might be the right thing to do if you want to use your equity for investments or sell the house.

The other problem was the credit card debt was so high on his credit report that borrowing for home improvements was out of the question. The kids still don't have a swimming pool.

The non-streamlined installment agreement or (NSIA)

If you owe over $50,000 to the IRS and want to pay installments, you may have to apply for a non-streamlined installment agreement (NSIA).

This payment plan requires you to provide detailed financial information to the IRS and negotiate a monthly payment amount to pay off your tax debt within the statute of limitations.

Some of the details of an NSIA are:

You can apply for an NSIA by phone, mail, or in person. You will need to show all your financial information, and I mean all of it. This is NOT the time to hide something from the IRS. You'll be committing a felony, and they will prosecute you.

They will ask you to offer a monthly payment based on your financial details. But it must be enough to pay the tax bill within the 10-year time limit. Whatever you offer, they are going to ask for more. Be ready to justify why your offer is as good as it gets.

They will look at the other collection alternatives, and if your monthly offer is the best deal they can get, they will take it. With your approval, these are negotiated settlements and payment plans managed by the collection agent and myself.

Now let's go back to the DIY taxpayer and how I would have negotiated his payoff plan.

First, I would have pointed out to the collection agent that he had less than $150,000 equity in his home so they could file a lien, but they could not force a sale under state law. I would have shown that the cars were on lease and had no value. His pension was small at less than $50,000, and it would be a long-drawn, out affair to seize the pension, leaving enough for the taxpayer to cover income taxes and penalty liabilities, so they may only end up with $30,000 if they were lucky.

Those financial details would have given me the ammunition to get the NSIA approved at $3,371 monthly, including interest. Then I would have recommended that he apply for the home improvement loan at a 30-year payout so his kids could have a horse barn and swimming pool. The payments would be around $1,850. I would also recommend that he apply for at least some credit cards to have a cushion to fall back on if something goes wrong. All that and his house, tax, and car payments would have totaled around $8,421 in monthly payments. That seems like a lot, but this guy was making $25,000 a month at his job, so he could swing the audit, pool, barn, cars and home - he could have it all if he kept his public record clear of tax liens.

Now I'm sure you're asking, "Why would anyone want to be in that kind of debt? It sure seems risky." Of course, I would have pointed that out, but I'm sure the pool and barn were worth the risk of being under such high monthly obligations.

None of this happened, by the way. He borrowed to pay the tax bill and gave up on the pool. Hopefully, he can refinance those credit cards in a year when the higher interest kicks in.

Summary:

If you understand the tax law, the IRS will not be able to push you around. Get ahead of their collection process, and you will manage your cash flow instead of some bureaucrat deciding how much you can get by.

As you might imagine, figuring out how to save your assets and make the tax settlement as painless as possible requires strategic planning and an understanding of the collection process. That's what I do for my clients.

Chapter 16:

What About Filing For Bankruptcy?

Should you just file for bankruptcy and let it all work out in the courts? First of all, I want you to know that bankruptcy is complicated, and you will not be able to make a decision based on this chapter. This is no DIY escape plan; it will be drawn out and expensive.

However, it is tempting. We all know more than one person that filed for bankruptcy got to keep their house and means of making a living, settled their debts for five and ten cents on the dollar paid over several years, and pretty soon everything seems to return to normal.

First, know this. Your credit report will drop between 200 and 300 points the day you file BK. The bankruptcy will stay on your public record for 7 to 10 years affecting your future ability to get a mortgage or buy a car at a decent credit rating. In the future, it may keep you from buying rental properties to offset your income tax with depreciation.

That does not mean you are dead in the water as you try to rebuild your financial fortress. Many businesspeople have filed for bankruptcy and gone on to build great businesses. Walt Disney is the most common example. Henry Ford is another household name. He filed twice before finally figuring out how to make cars at a profit.

Remember, everything ALWAYS works out. Don't panic. Make thoughtful decisions going forward and you'll be back on top in 3 to 5 years.

When should you use bankruptcy in tax resolution?

Generally, only when you are behind on all your other bills as well, not just taxes, so if your LLC finds itself with $75,000 in taxes due and you're behind another $50,000 in debt to your vendors, you may want to consider the BK route. But you should NEVER make this decision on your own. If we can get all your cards face up on the table, a strategy or two will start to become obvious, and you can decide then if I should bring in a BK lawyer to help you navigate the Federal courts.

What are the three common types of bankruptcies?

Chapter 7: This is the complete liquidation of all your assets. It's available for individuals as well as businesses. A court-appointed trustee will let you get out with your clothes, a low-value car and maybe some personal mementos. Everything else goes to a bankruptcy trustee to sell at auction or to a liquidator. The cash raised is then divided up between your creditors. The Federal BK Judge may determine if the payments to the IRS are enough to settle your tax obligations.

Bankruptcy will not get payroll trust fund taxes dismissed.

Now you may be able to get your home and pension exempted from the total liquidation. The rules, again, are complicated, and sometimes it's up to the judge to make a final decision.

As an individual, you may be able to file bankruptcy for $5,000 to $10,000. If you're filing as a business, the sky's the limit. I've had clients go this route only to find the cost went over a quarter million. However, Chapter 7 bankruptcy is cheaper than a long-drawn-out Chapter 11, where you try to save your business.

Chapter 11: This is for a business that wants to negotiate payments to creditors, predators and tax collectors. The idea is that your assets are added up, your liabilities are totaled, and the judge will rule that you must pay the difference over time. All the details are negotiated.

If you enter an installment agreement or offer in compromise and then file bankruptcy, the negotiated settlements with the IRS will be null and void. So don't negotiate a lower tax bill, then file bankruptcy; it won't work for you.

Chapter 13: It is the same as 11 but for individuals. Corporations of any type have to use chapter 11. That might mean you have to file two petitions, one personal and one for the business. Sole proprietors will use 13 to bundle the business and personal debt into one bucket and work on reducing the entire bucket.

There are two times when you might choose to go bankrupt

- A. You have no hope of salvaging anything from your finances and just need a clean slate to start over.
- B. The creditors, predators and tax collectors are closing in on all sides, and you just need a little more time and some protection to sort it all out.

Who should do the work for you?

If you are under attack (law suites, liens, levies and garnishments), you may need to file a bankruptcy petition right away to slow down the process. I will refer you to a local attorney I've worked with that understands what I do to get your tax bill cleared up. You'll need to give them a retainer and expect it to start in the $5,000 range.

I know you've seen those ads on TV that we can take you bankrupt for $695. But those are for people who defaulted on the loan for their TV and owed the cell phone carrier a few hundred dollars. If taxes are in the mix, the IRS will make it complicated.

As soon as your petition is filed, it is my turn to get to work. My bookkeepers will bill $120 an hour to reconstruct and fix your balance sheet. Accurate financial statements are going to be required by the judge. Then I will file all the back tax returns at $375 an hour. The returns are a requirement of the IRS, and they can stop your bankruptcy cold in its tracks if you don't comply.

With the tax returns filed, you, the bankruptcy lawyer, and I will devise a plan to submit to the court. There will be a lot of back and forth as the

IRS and creditors all jockey for favor with the judge.

Within the next year, you should have it all behind you. If you were lucky, you could keep your house because it did not have a large equity, and you may be able to save your pension. That should be enough to get back in the saddle to rebuild your financial fortress, but this time you'll be compliant and knowledgeable about how money and taxes work. It won't take long to say EVERYTHING ALWAYS WORKS OUT, finally.

Summary:

IS BANKRUPTCY RIGHT FOR YOU? I'm hoping the answer is no. It's expensive, can drag on for a long time, and the outcome is unpredictable because the judge will make the final decisions. Once they make a ruling, it requires an appeal to change their mind, and that just keeps the money and emotional drains open. We want to put all this behind you with as little damage as possible, but mostly we want to get it done quickly.

However, if we put all the cards on the table face up and you're in a pretty big hole, we will consider recommending it. Most of the time, it is not necessary to go bankrupt.

Chapter 17:

Can I Change My Name Or Move To Brazil? Can I Challenge The Law?

When you can't sleep worrying about the IRS, and it's been going on for months or maybe even years - your mind starts to wander into the green mist, and you come up with some unrealistic ideas.

The three most common yet unrealistic ideas I get are....

1. Can I go to Mexico, get some fake IDs, return to America as an immigrant, and start over under a new name?
2. What are my chances of slipping out of the country and never returning? Can I be a tax fugitive in Brazil?
3. Can we counter-sue the IRS? I heard that Congress did not actually ratify the 16th Amendment, so they can't legally ask me to pay, right?

Let's look at the reality of these ideas.

Can You Come Back From Mexico?

This may have been possible 25 years ago, but not anymore. Homeland Security has made it a lot tougher than you think. You are not going to blend in when you go to Mexico. The policia are going to spot you on your first day. If you are picked up, they will assume you are up to something illegal and throw the book at you. If the Mexican federales find you in the country illegally, they will throw you into jail for two years. I know that's funny. They can send millions of people to us, but we can't send one person to them.

If you find some fake IDs and make it back to the US border, Homeland

Security will interview and fingerprint you. You'll show up as an imposter in minutes and probably be incarcerated. You might even see your picture on Fox News from jail.

If you manage to get past all those hurdles, you might want to consider that the only work you'll ever be able to get is hard labor for cash. As soon as you try to get a good-paying job, you'll find you don't have the credentials the law requires to get work.

Overall I'd say you have about a 90% chance of ending up in Jail in Mexico or back in the US trying to become an immigrant.

Can I Slip Out Of The Country And Become A Fugitive?

Now this is something that has bafled me until I did the research for this book. You would think someone like Elizabeth Holmes (founder of Theranos), who we both know squirreled a ton of money away in some hidden bank, would just slip out of the country and disappear. She has brains, money and was facing 11 years in prison. I would think she would hide in some tropical paradise and never be heard from again. Yet she is locked up.

The truth is everyone who has tried to become a fugitive has ended up 'ratted out' by someone and got captured, or they ended up dead by mysterious circumstances. Remember, John McAfee was found dead in his prison cell in Spain. She is probably safer in a US prison than trying to be a fugitive.

Plus, there are only 21 countries that do not have an extradition treaty with the USA. The list includes countries like the Maldives, Cambodia, Laos and Nepal. Do you want to live there so you don't have to pay taxes?

Besides, here is something interesting: most countries don't want you, so you'll probably end up in prison anyway. In many countries, they don't need much of an excuse to put you in jail. Just ask Brittney Griner, the WNBA player who spent a year in a Russian prison. By the way, I'm glad she made it back, and I heard she no longer kneels when the national anthem plays.

Can I Sue The IRS Because The Amendment Was Not Ratified?

NO. The supreme court ruled in 1916 that the 16th Amendment was the law of the land. The income tax is legal no matter what you think. The IRS has never lost a case questioning the legality of the tax law. Don't waste your time.

Can I Walk Away And Ignore The Entire Collection Process?

Yes, if you file your returns. Remember that not paying your taxes won't get you in prison, but not filing your returns will. Also, lying to the IRS about your income or assets will get you in jail.

But if you want to just ignore every letter and collection effort they throw at you, you can. Be aware they will seize your home and every other asset they can find, so you are walking away with nothing. Those seizures will go on for a long time, so you have given up your 2nd chance to build a financial fortress for your family.

One Last Story About Lying.

When the IRS asks you about an asset or income stream, they almost always know the answer beforehand. They are trying to trick you into lying to them. If you don't feel comfortable talking to the collection agent, hire me, that is what I do. Plus, I won't accidentally blurt out something that will come back to haunt you.

In Wyoming, about 15 years ago, an elderly couple failed to report the sale of some jewelry that had been in the family for a long time. The couple got audited for some reason, and the $100,000 in cash showed up as unreported income. The couple was angry about the IRS trying to get a piece of the sale. They needed the money to live on and thought it was unfair that they would be asked to pay capital gains tax on something that had been in the family for over 30 years.

Well, I guess they must have made the collection agent angry because he started interviewing them on assets and such to file liens and, eventually, levies so he could collect the taxes.

The couple forgot to mention that they had $600,000 in an investment account in the Caribbean. Well the IRS knew because they had wired money into the account over the years, leaving an electronic transaction record. The elderly couple figured that it was secret for some reason.

So the revenue agent brought federal perjury charges against the couple for failing to disclose the account. Do you know that both the 76 yr. old husband and 74-year-old wife were sent to Federal prison for 18 months?

You would have thought the media would have had such a sad event all over the paper. But today's media favors a heavy-handed Federal government; plus, being from Wyoming, I'm sure the couple was conservative. So the press decided that no one needed to hear about it. Now I believe it was an overreach on the part of the IRS. The kind of behavior a tax resolution expert can stop in its tracks.

Summary:

We probably watch too much television in America, which gives us ideas about slipping off the radar. It will not go well for you. It is far easier to settle with the IRS, go through a few years of painful payments, and be done with it all. Get it behind you and back in the saddle, building your financial fortress.

Everything works out unless we do something stupid.

Chapter 18: *Payroll Taxes*

The first time I realized that the IRS believes they have eminent domain and anything inside the borders of our country belongs to them was a number of years ago.

On a summer day in 2012, I saw firsthand how the IRS believes anything inside the borders of our country ultimately belongs to the government. The pure definition of eminent domain.

The IRS philosophy was, and probably still is, you get to use your money, house and boat that you earned, but only until we take it away from you. I learned about all this from my buddy Steve, who I played racquetball with a few times weekly.

Steve was a pretty successful salesman; by age 31, he already had a 4,000-square-foot house in a gated community. The local newspaper coined the big box houses as McMansions. Now that big of a home is no big deal today, but it was pretty fancy back then. I was hopeful that I could afford a McMansion one day.

Steve calls me and says, "Hey, I know you're an accountant; I'd like you to come by after dinner. I want to get your take on something that happened to me today."

Later after a cold one, Steve opens up. He tells me, "Today I came home a little early, the kids were still in school, but there was a strange car in my driveway, and the garage was open. I was scared something might be wrong, so I ran inside to check on Amber."

At that moment, my heart stopped, I had no idea where the story was going, but I had watched enough TV drama to know this is usually how bad news starts. I'm glad I kept my mouth shut because Steve began talking again.

Steve says, "I ran in the house, and Amber is at the kitchen table. She just looks up at me and says, "You need to go out in the garage right now and figure this out."

Upon entering the garage, Steve saw a pudgy, poorly dressed middle-aged man with a clipboard writing down a list of Steve's tools, garden tractor and his wife's car. Knowing Steve, it was no surprise, but he told me his first inclination was to pick up a shovel and get the hard part done first; there would be time for questions later.

Before anything could happen, the intruder pulled out a badge and announced he was from the IRS. Now Steve is totally confused. His taxes were current, and he hadn't seen a collection letter or any other correspondence from the IRS since that stunt he pulled right out of college.

"What is this all about?." Steve asked.

Well, you are behind on your payroll taxes for the last six months. You owe the IRS $2,890. The little man explained that I'm trying to figure out what you own so I can send it to a tax auction to pay that debt. If you don't owe the bank too much on your wife's' car, I see enough stuff in here to raise the three grand.

Steve tells me that he was calm enough to ask some sane questions. He knew the agent was at the wrong house or had made some kind of error.

The agent started asking Steve about a company called Silver Cow

Advertising. "Do you own that business?" Steve replied, "No, that belongs to a friend of mine; I loaned him $10,000 to get it started a year and a half ago. Come to think of it, he hasn't made his payments in a while. What is going on?" You may not own it, but your name is on the signature card for the company checking account. That means you are responsible for the unpaid payroll taxes. Steve was pretty surprised by that news. He had forgotten about helping his friend set up the bank account long ago.

The agent asked if Steve could give him a check for $2,890.00 right now and close it all out. When Steve said no, the guy went to a new sheet on his clipboard and started asking Steve about his income and expenses. He wanted to know where Steve and Amber banked and whether they owned any cash-value life insurance.

At this point, Steve is a little scared and says, "I will bring a check down to your office on Friday." The pudgy fellow reminds Steve that until these taxes are caught up, everything in his bank was the property of the IRS. His paycheck belonged to the IRS, and everything in the garage was ours as well. If you want to keep it, don't forget to be at my office at 9 AM sharp. With that, he waddled away, looking pretty smug and drove off.

Steve then looked at me and said, "What do you make of all that?" Well, I answered, from what I've heard in the training classes I had been to, you need to do two things tomorrow. Go to the bank and draw a $2,890 cashier's check made out to the IRS. Then get your name off that signature card. I'm not sure what you need to do about your friend's business, but I suggest you get your name off everything that has anything to do with that company, or you're going to get dragged into an even bigger mess down the road.

From Steve's details, I came to understand that the IRS does not take lightly anyone who fails to forward payroll taxes collected in trust. Steve didn't know anything about the taxes not being paid, but since his name was associated with the account, he got nailed. My guess is the little collection agent had already failed to collect from the responsible party, so Steve became the deep pockets that could clear up the mess.

WHAT DID STEVE AND I LEARN FROM THIS EPISODE?

First, the tax resolution for payroll taxes is harder than income tax. The standards for an offer in compromise or installment plan are tougher than not paying enough on your 1040.

Second: Don't fail to pay your payroll taxes. It's an easy loan for most business owners. Skip one week, thinking you'll catch up next week. But that almost never happens. When Steve started his business the following year, one of the first vendors he hired was a reputable payroll company that drew the taxes out of his operating account every week and sent them to the IRS. One trip to the garage was enough for him.

The Taxpayers Bill Of Rights

Today the IRS has to be a little more kind. We covered this in chapters one and two, but much of the evil commander thinking still goes inside the IRS chambers.

WHAT IS THE TFRP?

Payroll trust fund delinquencies are income tax and FICA (Social Security and Medicare) withholdings from employees' wages. The IRS requires businesses to collect these federal taxes on trust. If an employer fails to do so, the IRS can hold the employer and any responsible person personally liable for a trust fund recovery penalty equal to the unpaid trust fund taxes (TFRP)

Bankruptcy does not discharge payroll trust fund delinquencies. Even if you file for bankruptcy as an individual or a business, the TFRP can still be assessed against you. Thus, bankruptcy will not eliminate payroll trust fund delinquencies or the TFRP. For specific advice, consult a tax professional or bankruptcy attorney.

Will You Be Able To Use The Offer In Compromise With TFRP Funds?

The IRS prioritizes payroll trust fund accounts and considers them a matter of public trust, making OICs difficult to obtain. You must file all tax returns, make all estimated tax payments, and not be under audit or litigation to qualify for an OIC. You must also show that you doubt your liability, ability to pay, or an exceptional circumstance that makes paying your full tax debt unfair or inequitable.

Despite meeting these requirements, the IRS may reject your OIC. The IRS will assess your offer based on income, expenses, assets, liabilities, and future earnings. The IRS will consider your offer's public policy effects, such as encouraging taxpayers to comply or undermining the tax system. Thus, payroll trust fund OICs are rare and difficult.

That part meant that you might end up as *Ensign Expendable* and become an example for others to learn from.

Well, Then, What About The Statute Of Limitations?

Unpaid payroll trust fund accounts have different statutes of limitations for employers and a responsible person. A responsible person can sometimes be the bookkeeper who does the payroll. If she can sign checks and the taxes go unpaid, your little bookkeeper making $18 an hour could get hit with tens of thousands in payroll taxes. She will be held personally responsible for it. Her family will suffer greatly, and she does not have the resources to recover from such a nightmare as you do. In other words, it is evil to do something like that to an innocent employee.

Most bookkeepers know they can get screwed if you're not making payroll tax deposits. That's why most refuse to be on the signature card.

The statute runs out in three years for your bookkeeper. However, for the boss, the statute is ten years.

The responsible party in your business will be anyone with an ownership position, and they can sign checks. That mostly means the owner and spouse. There is no innocent spouse relief for TFRP problems.

Overall this is a very serious problem.

So What Can Be Done?

First and foremost, you have very little time to deal with trust fund taxes. The IRS can walk into your business without warning and close you down at any time. They will simply announce to all your employees that you can no longer pay them, which should just about be the end of your company.

Installments To Pay Off TFRP Obligations.

If you come to me with TFRP problems, my first step will be to talk to the collection agent and explain that, as of today, you will be using a reputable payroll company and all trust fund monies will be collected and forwarded on time. That will happen TODAY. I'll find the right payroll service for you; I have a good relationship with the local ones who are substantial enough that we can trust them to do what they say.

Then I will negotiate a 30 to 60-day cooling-off period to determine your next best course of action. It is doubtful that you will pay these taxes at some kind of discount or be able to run the clock out with the statute of limitations.

Based on your gross revenue and profit margins, I'll make an offer/proposal to pay off the back taxes over ten years. They will probably not accept my offer but come back with a 2 or 3-year payout proposal. You will be in the loop and have the final say on what can be done.

We can try the OIC, but the chances are not good that you will be approved. The IRS is very serious about trust funds being used by the business to cover daily operating expenses. That is just the harsh cold fact of it.

What If You Have Been Paying Your Employees On 1099?

Suppose you've been questioned about the contractor classification for your employees. The IRS tells you to convert to W2s and start withholding taxes. You have three choices.

A) Close your business and quit.

B) Comply and hire a payroll company today.

C) Ask for an administrative hearing and convince the judge that your people are 1099 workers.

The way employers get caught is through complaints from their employees. Imagine I'm a roofer on one of your crews and made $75,000 last year. Suddenly, the IRS wants $15,000 for income taxes and self-employment taxes to cover social security and Medicare.

Your employee is not going to blame themselves for failing to hold a little back each month. That employee is going to lay 100% of the blame on you. The IRS is going to follow up on the complaint.

They have a set of 21 questions they ask about your employer/employee relationship. If your business fails the test, they will come after you. By the way, they did the 21 questions with your employee; they already know the answer when you get the letter.

This is a nightmare scenario because the IRS can ask you to pay your employee's tax bills for the past one or two, or even more years. They will tell you it should have been paid all along; you are liable since you did not do it.

I talked to an accountant in Washington, DC, who told me about a contractor that misclassified his employees for eight years and was handed a 1.5-million-dollar invoice. The guy is 68 yrs. old. It's a disaster.

Summary:

I hate to tell you this, but payroll taxes are not a joke. They are difficult to excuse. Impossible to bankrupt out of, and the IRS will come after you with both barrels blazing.

If you are concerned about the employment status of your workforce, it is not a time to put it off. Call me at the office today, and let's review the 21 questions and how you have structured your control over the people working for you.

Will Everything Work Out Even With TFRP Problems?

Yes, because in most cases, you'll get nailed within 90 days. Income taxes can take years for the audit or non-filer status to reach the top of the monthly collection agents' list of cases.

Payroll trust funds are at the top of the list within months. Luckily the IRS won't let you get too far down the rabbit hole. The good news is that once you suffer this problem, you'll be like Steve and engage a payroll service from now on. No more chances.

One last payroll tax story because it is so interesting.

In 2014 I attended a seminar on how to buy distressed businesses, fix the problems and flip the company at a profit. One of the speakers told us about his best deal.

A home healthcare company in Arizona had somehow managed to get into the IRS for one million dollars of unpaid payroll taxes. I have no idea how the bill ever got that big. Our speaker told us that he got a call from a friend telling him to get to Arizona on the next flight; he could probably buy the three million-a-year company for a song.

After listening to the owners for an hour, he realized the song would be a siren song, and anyone who bought this business would be a shipwreck by morning.

The IRS had already announced they were seizing the business on Monday, and it was Friday night. The owners wanted the potential buyer to put up the one million for the taxes in exchange for 49% of the company. So they would still be in charge. The same people who killed the company thought they should keep running it. Go figure.

The owner had inherited the business from her father, and over two years, she brilliantly moved the business from six million a year in revenue to three million. They were losing money hand over fist, and on Monday, they would be D.O.A.

There was no way I would do this deal. But the company had three million in contracts of which one-third were profitable.

So here is what he offered them. He pulled an envelope from his left pocket and showed the owner $5,000 in cash. He had an envelope in the other pocket with $10,000, but he knew that was more than he would need to get what he wanted.

He told the owner I don't want your company; it will be gone on Monday." But here is what I do want. I will give you this envelope with $5,000. What you do with the cash is up to you.

In exchange, I want you to provide me with a list of all your employees who provide home health care around the metro area, and I want a copy of every contract from patients for your services.

There is something called a bulk transfer rule. If you buy more than 50% of a business's assets, you also get that business's liabilities. But if you just buy a list of employees and customers with no established worth, you can get the most valuable asset in the company without the tax debt.

The owner grabbed the envelope and went to their computer to print the customer and employee lists.

The speaker then got on the phone and called every competent salesperson he could think of and promised them $5,000 for two days' work if they could be in Arizona in the morning. Six showed up, and they mapped out all the customers' and employees' homes and went out to each one of the 'good' ones, which only amounted to about ⅓ of the business. The rest of the customers were bid so low they were causing losses.

The overnight team explained to each employee what was happening and 'You still have a job.' They told the patients they still had the same caregiver and pricing. All you need to do is sign this new contract.

By Monday, they had a brand new one million-dollar-a-year business, with a new name, no tax liability from a bulk transfer of the old company, and six salesmen went back to the airport with $5,000 in their pocket.

This has nothing to do with tax resolution, but I guess I told you about it because it was all driven by the failure to deposit the trust funds collected from the employee paychecks.

If you fail to stay current on your payroll taxes, some smart operator may also pick through the bones of your business. Payroll taxes are not a joke.

Chapter 19:

Will I Recover Financially And Get Back On Top?

When I sat down with Jose for coffee, it had been six years since I had helped him get out of trouble with the IRS. We had a weekly meeting ever since to review his finances, taxes and investments. He paid me handsomely for the one hour of advice; I think that was because he learned during the tax collection disaster that he knew a lot about running a machine shop but not much about how money and taxes work.

He paid for coffee, saying you know I'm already worth double what I was six years ago when those *guys* wiped me out. I wasn't sure what that word meant, but I smiled anyway. What excited me was that he talked about his 'net-worth', not his gross sales or net income. I knew he had come a long way if he was thinking about wealth instead of income.

Jose said, "When the mierda hit the fan, I was wiped out. I thought my life was over." It took me 30 years to build that machine shop, buy my family home, and get the boat and the King Ranch F-350. In under a year, it was gone. But as you know, instead of starting over from scratch, I learned from you that I could probably buy some retiring machinists and be right back where we were. It worked. I found a shop for sale, and it came with everything I needed, plus six good employees. Well, I still had my customer list from before, so I bought the shop, used the profits to make the payments and then went back to all my old customers and sold them on trying me again. I was able to double the business within six months. The down payment was tough, but that hard money lender got me into the building and the company. Thank God, I have him paid back; 10% interest was a killer." All the time he was talking, I was still trying to figure out what mierda meant.

"Then my wife found a nice house on two acres that was in foreclosure. It was in terrible condition, but my kids are old enough now that I'm teaching them construction skills by rehabbing the house as we live in it. Zillow says the house is now worth double what I paid for it now."

"But you know the biggest thing to change; I'm not trying to impress anyone now. Today, I'm driving an old Dodge, and the $1,500 a month in truck payments I used to make goes into my pension. This year the business I bought will be paid for, and I'll start buying some rentals with that $4,000 a month, so my tax bill won't be as high going forward because of the depreciation."

"I'm not going to make the same mistakes as before. I was a rugged individualist, and it cost me dearly. I spent way too much time buying stuff I did not need, with money I did not have, to impress people I did not like. On top of that, I turned my old accountant down when he offered to help me understand my cash flow and tax liabilities. I said no to the lawyer that wanted to create some trust to protect my assets, and I ran the financial planner off when he started talking about life insurance and pension plans. Today's tax laws, accounting rules, and legal environment are too complicated for an old Jose like me; I will seek expert advice from now on."

Joses' story is common. But not everyone gets wiped out. Most of the time, we just need to get some reasonable payment plan in place, and you can get on with your life.

My primary job is to get your tax problems out of your head. I take the collection calls, I read the letters, I negotiate with the IRS, and you focus on what you do well.

When I tell my clients that they will be way better off once we have them through their tax resolution, they always look at me and say something like, 'Right, it took me 20 years to get where I'm at, and I'm about to lose it all." Everyone who gets those ugly letters lives in fear of losing it all. That's' a heavy load to shoulder.

But here are the facts. If you are brave, focused and a good student of money, you can attract wealth pretty fast in America as long as you live in the service of others.

So my answer to worried clients is it took you 20 years to get where you are, but every step was a college class in hard knocks. You've made more mistakes than you can remember, and you had to learn how to do everything, like start a business, keep a customer happy, buy a house, and hire an employee; the list is probably five pages long of important steps you took for the first time and failed at it more than once.

This time you already know how to do all that stuff. Now you can get things done a lot faster. Plus, you know what NOT to waste your time on. What-not-to-do is probably the biggest asset you have. You'll be able to cut the time back to your current station in life by 50% just because you know where to focus. That means your 20 just became 10 years to return to where you are now.

A life run by focusing on accurate numbers is a prosperous life. But it gets better. You received a master's degree from the IRS on why you should pay attention to the tax laws and your financials. So, you're down to 5 years to return to where you started with a financial guardian angel like me helping you along the way. That 10 years could be shaved in half.

But it gets even better. Once you have focus and financial control, you can start growing your life back using other people's money. That means buying appreciating assets with borrowed money that offers depreciation that will offset your income tax bill. That is what rich people do.

That means you could be back in place in as little as three years or maybe six, like Jose. To get there, you must follow the adage, "If you work for five years like others won't, you will live the rest of your life like others can only dream about." But hard work is not the entire answer. A key ingredient to success is a willingness to seek and accept advice and counsel from people who understand money, investing, taxes and credit.

Pretty cool.

But that won't be the end of it. If you learn the lessons about money and taxes, you'll realize that the complicated tax code was developed to encourage you to build wealth. Those who understand that get rich. In a decade, you could end up being ten times more successful than your old path was taking you.

Please don't take that as an insult; we both know you were sloppy or would not have gotten into trouble in the first place. But your days of being sloppy must come to an end. Unforeseen events probably caused your tipping point, but you were not protected behind a financial fortress, so normal life events brought you down. My dad would say, "Get over it and get back in the saddle."

However, all my predictions about how well you will do are based on one question, WILL YOU LEARN? The dangerous part is that God keeps repeating lessons until we learn them. From now on, learn from your mistakes and the mistakes of others and keep away from sloppy behavior.

Do you need to hire someone like me?

Can you do all the tax negotiations and strategy on your own? Well, here is something you must know if you're trying to save money. Your government is duplicitous, and they will not tell you the best steps to take.

The tax collection agent wants to get your case closed and off the books as fast as possible with the coldest hard cash collected as they can get. They will not outright lie to you. But not telling you all your rights or the minimum they might accept to make a settlement is not telling the truth and the whole truth.

Unfortunately, proving government lies is hard. We must be sharp to catch the government's well-crafted words and rules written by highly paid lawyers.

Fortunately, their lies about the law are based on simple deceptions. They use the sin of omission to mislead you into false assumptions or overreporting.

Governments never lie directly. That would be too easy to discover, and government employees value their pensions and benefits too much to risk termination for more money for the boss.

Instead, the government uses deceptive "legal terms" that you don't understand, and you're unaware that the "words" you're reading are "legal terms" that the government has defined to mean something completely different than what you think they mean in plain English.

Most Americans think government documents are meant to clarify matters. The opposite is true. The government uses "jurisdictional context" to confuse Americans.

What does all this mean? In the dozens of client stories I've shared with you here, every single time, the collection agent initially asked for evidence they did not need or left the taxpayer believing he was in bigger trouble than they were.

It's an age-old tactic of using fear to get you to fork over more money faster. So the question is - do you need professional help?

Yes - I have been standing up for clients in front of the IRS for years. I know pretty much what they will accept, and I've got a good idea of what kind of wool they might try to pull over your eyes.

My mother used to tell me, 'There are no accidents' if something bad happened to you, it was because of a decision you made 1 minute or one year before the accident.

It was not until I was an adult that I realized how right she was. Getting nailed by the IRS is unfortunate, but something we got involved in or did caused our name to pop up on their radar.

Am I Expensive?

Of course, I am; I'm good at what I do. If you end up paying me $5,000 and you get to keep your house, I'd say that was a bargain. If you end up paying me $10,000 and it takes me two years to get an offer in compromise approved, but you get out of paying $100,000 in taxes, I'd say that was a bargain.

I'm not giving you a price here because I have no idea of your problem's scope. That would be like calling your auto mechanic and asking how much it costs to start your car. You will not get an answer because they don't know if the battery is dead, or the crankshaft is broken; they will give you a price after they look at the car.

The Final Word

Through these stories, you've realized I have a wide swath of experience of standing up to the IRS on your behalf.

But the more important point to know is EVERYTHING WORKS OUT. If the poor guy who flew his plane into the IRS building had just known that there is life after resolving your tax problems, he would have walked his daughter down the aisle on her wedding day.

If the lawyer in Massachusetts had not tried to negotiate with the IRS by himself, he would have been treated better, and the agent would have been reassigned long before the taxpayer let the carbon monoxide in his garage put him to sleep forever.

If the taxpayer panicked and sold his home without realizing the Florida homestead act protected it, his wife would not have left him.

First and foremost, I want to get the tax problems out of your head. I will take the calls and read the letters. If you wake up in a cold sweat at 3 AM and can't get back to sleep from worry, you are not working at full capacity. Let me have the worry so that you can have the sleep of the angels.

I will lay out all your options based on turning your cards face up on the table in my office. Once we have strategy A and a plan B worked out, I'll go to bat for you and get the IRS to approve your workout.

We always come up with a resolution. It may not be 100% of what I ask for, but the IRS wants your case closed, so they will negotiate. This nightmare will end so you can get on with your life.

After we have a solution and you're ready to get busy rebuilding your financial fortress, we can talk about asset protection, high-profit business management, investments and tax planning so you never have to worry about this again.

Let's get together for an hour and see if we like each other and if I think I can help. That starts with a free consultation to go over your problem. Call my office at 833-477-4911, and we'll schedule a convenient time for your most pressing questions. Have the list ready and hit me hard.

Thank You

Marc Boulanger CPA

PS When you look back in 10 years, you may say, *'That tax problem was the best thing that ever happened to me.'* Won't that be amazing?

www.ingramcontent.com/pod-product-compliance
Lightning Source LLC
Chambersburg PA
CBHW071830210526
45479CB00001B/75